MW00629107

PREDICTABLE RESULTS

PREDICTABLE RESULTS

HOW **SUCCESSFUL COMPANIES** TACKLE **GROWTH CHALLENGES** *and* WIN

PATRICK THEAN · CHRIS COSPER · ALAN GEHRINGER
TIFFANY CHEPUL · BARRY PRUITT · CATHY MCCULLOUGH
LIZ MCBRIDE · TED SKINNER · MELISSA ENRIQUEZ

Published by Leadline, LLC
Charlotte, North Carolina

Copyright © 2017 by Rhythm Systems, Inc.

Cover and book design by Paul Barrett of
Girl Friday Productions and Kim Lance
Cover image © Maydaymayday/iStockphoto.com

ISBN (hardcover): 978-0-9978257-1-8
e-ISBN: 978-0-9978257-2-5

Printed in the United States of America

We dedicate this book to our families, who are a blessing, especially Pei-Yee, Joe, Vera, John, Marsha, Brady, Mike, Emily, and Adriana. Thank you for your love, support, and patience.

In remembrance of our friend, Igor

CONTENTS

ACKNOWLEDGMENTS

This is an amazing book and it took a village. We started this project with the vision of sharing stories of success from our clients and our dream team at Rhythm Systems. I thought, *We have nine authors, so it's going to be easier and faster, right?* Wrong! This beautiful work with nine authors actually took more writing, more editing, and more project management and coordination than we had ever imagined. It turned out to be very challenging and rewarding to weave the work of nine authors into one book that would be enjoyable to read.

I want to thank Jessica Wishart, our project director and master cat herder. Jessica was able to bring the entire project team (writers and editors) along for this journey and make sure that our content was consistent. It took a very unique individual with writing and project-management skills to pull everything together and deliver this project. Thank you to Cindy Praeger, who worked with every author to bring out the best in our case studies. I also want to thank Lari Bishop, our editor extraordinaire, who helped us to express our individual passion and made it a cohesive work. All nine authors greatly appreciate Jessica, Cindy, and Lari for their work on our book.

Finally, we would like to thank our clients. It is a privilege to work with each of you, and we appreciate the opportunity to be part of your journey. We are especially grateful to our clients who shared their stories of growth challenges and breakthroughs for this book. We thank you for your willingness to be open and allow others to learn from your experiences using Rhythm to grow your business. Following is a list of these clients we would like to thank:

Arbill: Under the leadership of CEO Julie Copeland, Arbill's products and services are designed with one goal in mind: keeping workers safe. In order to achieve their vision of a world where every single worker makes it home safely after every single shift, Arbill is focused on innovating safety products and the way safety services are delivered. They strive to help companies control costs, engineer out safety risks, and minimize exposure to safety-related claims while protecting every worker. They provide safety training, consulting, technology, services, and personal protective equipment to businesses and government agencies. Arbill.com.

BioPlus Specialty Pharmacy: BioPlus is a national award-winning specialty pharmacy, currently providing pharmaceutical care to more than 6,000 patients per month. BioPlus has the skilled people and innovative technology to make it easy to refer and measurably improve the outcomes of patients facing complex chronic health conditions, such as bleeding disorders, hepatitis C, cancer, Crohn's disease, and rheumatoid arthritis. BioPlus is led by CEO and founder Dr. Stephen Vogt. Bioplusrx.com.

Boston Centerless: Serving customers all over the world in a variety of industries, Boston Centerless is the industry leader in precision grinding technology and is known for the manufacturing and distribution of precision bar materials. For end products as varied as spinal implants and aerospace valves, they provide solutions to customers that enhance their manufacturing processes. Steve Tamasi, CEO, leads the charge to deliver outstanding value and unmatched downstream savings to customers. Bostoncenterless.com.

EMC Precision: Founded in 1925 as a family-operated precision machining company, EMC Precision honors the principles behind four generations of success pursued with a steady eye on the future. Led by CEO Jeff Ohlemacher, EMC Precision's constant pursuit of excellence in manufacturing precision-machined parts is grounded in values of integrity, teamwork, and service to all stakeholders. EMC is committed to continuous investment in training, equipment, processes, engineering, and people, and the result is that they deliver custom products on time, defect-free, at the lowest cost, with exceptional customer satisfaction. Emcprecision.com.

Flexfab: With world-class manufacturing facilities located in the United States, Europe, South America, and China, Flexfab is a global leader in the manufacture of high-performance silicone and other advanced polymer products. Set apart by their cutting-edge technology, engineering expertise, and innovative R&D laboratory, Flexfab is devoted to delivering exceptional experiences to their customers in the aerospace, automotive, heavy-duty truck, rail, and industrial markets. Under the leadership of CEO Matt DeCamp, their focus is to provide excellence, value, and innovative solutions to their partners. Flexfab.com.

Inergex: A leader in service innovation, Inergex (now **Crossfuze**) has operations in Salt Lake City, New York City, and Buffalo in the United States; Toronto and Ottawa in Canada; and Manila in the Philippines. They work alongside IT leaders to help reshape services across their enterprise by building high-impact platforms powered by ServiceNow. These platforms are designed to provide visibility and automation that drive efficiency and governance. Their investment in R&D accelerates service and innovation outcomes and is underpinned by best practices that have been proven time and time again to deliver a best-in-class client experience. Crossfuze.com.

Infobip: With a platform touching over 60 percent of the world's mobile numbers, Infobip has built the largest network for enterprise mobile messaging around the globe. Having over 50 offices worldwide and billions of messages processed every month, they've worked tirelessly to create seamless mobile interactions between businesses and people through text messages, push notifications, emails, and chat apps. Led by CEO Silvio Kutic, their unique culture fuels continuous innovation and service quality and has resulted in top industry standing as the leading provider of mobile communication services. Infobip.com.

MarketLinc: Working under the leadership of CEO Don Simpson, MarketLinc enables ecommerce businesses to profitably capture up to 20 percent more revenue by delivering real-time, live sales assistance to high-potential visitors, precisely when help is needed. Powered by proprietary analytics and attribution capabilities, the MarketLinc Intelligent Visitor Engagement solution combines digital and live sales engagement to convert high-potential visitors before they abandon a site. MarketLinc's proven solution delivers breakthrough results for global brands and requires no upfront budget, and the unique pay-for-performance model means clients only pay for the incremental revenue generated. Marketlinc.com.

MobilityWorks: MobilityWorks is a national chain of certified wheelchair-accessible van providers. They have more than 70 showrooms across the country and offer a large selection of wheelchair vans and assistance from a staff of trained experts to better meet the needs of their customers. The company is led by CEO Bill Koeblitz and president Eric Mansfield. Mobilityworks.com.

North Shore Pediatric Therapy: North Shore Pediatric Therapy is the thought leader in pediatric therapy, providing evidence-based, individualized approaches to maximize each child's potential. Their experienced and innovative therapists are dedicated to helping children blossom and are motivated by their respect and love for kids. North Shore Pediatric Therapy warmly supports their families every step of the way. Their team offers nine specialties under one roof—neuropsychology, occupational therapy, physical therapy, speech therapy, applied behavior analysis (ABA), social work, school advocacy services, nutrition, and academic tutoring—with nine locations conveniently located throughout the Chicagoland and Milwaukee area. The company was built by founder Deborah Michael and is run by CEO Maria Hammer. Nspt4kids.com.

World Emblem: Led by CEO Randy Carr, World Emblem is one of the world's leading global suppliers of high-quality apparel decorations, including custom embroidered, sublimated, and digitally printed patches, high-visibility striping, transfers, name badges, FlexStyle, and various other products. World Emblem's high product quality is complemented by their ability to integrate sales, marketing, and operational functions to provide only the highest level of customer satisfaction with one of the quickest turn times in the industry. True to their name, World Emblem's five strategically placed national locations are supplemented by an additional three international locations ready to bring your brands to life. Worldemblem.com.

THE WINNING FORMULA FOR PREDICTABLE RESULTS

Have you ever had days when you've felt like your hair was on fire? If you're a leader in a growing company, the answer is likely yes. Growth can easily cause chaos, which leads to confusion and reactivity. At Infobip, not only were they growing fast, they also had a culture and a strategy for hypergrowth. They had a brilliant team, plenty of resources, a global footprint, a wide-open market, and so many great ideas. The company was achieving success after success, and the leaders knew they had the potential to achieve even more with the agile, can-do culture already deeply rooted in the company identity. But they also knew the pace could create chaos and burnout if they weren't proactive. They needed to figure out how to successfully prioritize and execute the right, and the biggest, opportunities. They needed their people focused and aligned around achieving goals that were clear and specific. They needed a way to harness the energy, connect all the dots, and manage the complexity.

Infobip is a global force in the programmable mobile messaging market. Have you ever received a text message or notification from an application, such as a social media app? If so, chances are that the message was processed by Infobip's systems and delivered to your phone through their global messaging infrastructure. In 2016 alone, their proprietary platform interacted with over 60 percent of all active mobile numbers in the world. With unsurpassed connectivity, it has the capacity to reach more than 6 billion mobile subscribers in 190 countries.

Amazingly, despite their rapid progress, one of their operating principles is "We have to go much, much, much, much *faster*." Founded in 2005, Infobip built an innovative technology platform, built an even better one two years later, launched a more robust one three years after that for enterprise clients, and continued improving and innovating from there. In 2009, they opened their global headquarters in London to support their rapidly growing international business structure. In 2010, they established regional hubs in Kuala Lumpur, Johannesburg, and Buenos Aires. By the time we met them in late 2014, they had 825 employees in 35 offices around the world, with a presence on most continents. After one of the first meetings with the Infobip leaders, our head of consulting, Chris Cosper, told our team she could feel the vibration of ideas speeding past her at 200 miles per hour. They wanted to do everything, and they wanted to do it fast.

Infobip has a growth trajectory and market position many of us might envy. Yet the leaders faced the same fundamental challenge as the leaders of any other midmarket company. They were getting by, from a management perspective, but the challenges were eating away at resources and opening the door to misalignment, which can be a drag on growth. Every one of their ten global regions was responsible for establishing, tracking, and reporting their own measures or key performance indicators (KPIs). Those measures were not standardized company-wide and didn't necessarily tie into the measures that mattered most to the executive team at headquarters. What were the real measures of success? How could the executive team compare performance, scale successes, and create synergy among these independent regions? Silos were growing within the regions, which led to duplicate work happening more and more often. Their ideas for

THE WINNING FORMULA FOR PREDICTABLE RESULTS † 3

growth were boundless, but their ability to prioritize strategically and execute at all leadership levels definitely needed improvement. Silvio Kutic—an engineer and programmer who developed the early platform, cofounded the company, and is now the CEO—recognized that they needed to find the optimal framework to support their complex and dynamic organization in order to realize their company's growth potential. Silvio was wise to see that sometimes you have to slow down first in order to go fast.

Just like you, the leaders at Infobip needed to overcome these common obstacles to get more of the right strategic things done and maintain growth in a predictable way. It doesn't matter whether the growth you're aiming for is 20 percent or 80 percent. Growth of all kinds presents the unique paired challenges of greater complexity and uncertainty, and keeping teams focused and aligned seems to become increasingly difficult. You need a way to marshal your forces to make your initiatives happen and to build the visibility that will help you know if you're on the right path. You need the execution rhythm, discipline, and perseverance to overcome—or avoid—the common obstacles to growth again and again. Because when you can do that, you'll grow your company faster, your results will be more predictable, and you'll be happier.

Achieving that level of discipline and consistency is not easy, but Infobip's leaders were determined. Like everything else they tackled, once they found the approach and platform they felt could help them solve their challenges, they moved on all fronts at once. The Rhythm team worked with Infobip's executive team to establish the key performance indicators they believed would help them track the company's success: interactions, traffic, revenue, number of locations, and a few others—a refined and focused list. They set up dashboards to track weekly so they could be proactive versus reactive. The business development team, which was made up of representatives from all ten regions, was given the responsibility of analyzing and validating the

KPIs, establishing appropriate targets for each region, discussing how to consistently report the numbers in a way that would accurately roll up into the executive-level composite measure, etcetera, so they could get the right information from the people that knew the most. Visibility, consistency, and clarity in key regional projects improved dramatically. And with a collaborative platform in place to support Infobip's strategy and communication, teams were able to work cross regionally and cross functionally. This organizational development was one of the important steps in the regional growth the company has achieved.

With Igor Sigmundovic, scrum master and head of coaching at Infobip, as the driver, leaders at the executive and regional level committed to planning every quarter to bring strategic focus to the work of their dispersed teams. Working with their Rhythm consultant, they focused on top priorities they could get done with their resources, instead of creating a plan that included every great idea. After the first round of quarterly planning for all ten regions resulted in 85 priorities for the company's leaders, they understood they would need to improve their prioritization and alignment skills the next quarter, and the next, and the next. They had to be selective. Today, they more consistently set a realistic number of priorities every quarter (although they're still always very ambitious), and with the right energy devoted to each, they successfully achieve more.

Using the weekly dashboards, Infobip was able to leverage their ability to track priorities across teams and regions, and brought focus and efficiency to key initiatives. Strategic partnerships with mobile providers and others in the telecom industry are the lifeblood of their business. To build those partnerships around the world, they need a local presence in many different regions or countries. Opening new offices and creating local legal entities are a necessity, but it's an onerous process (especially outside the US or Europe) involving efforts from legal, operations, administration, and more. Establishing company- and department-level priorities, setting KPIs, and tracking progress weekly has helped them adjust each time, refine the process, and shorten the timeline. Standardizing this process with a repeatable set of priorities and KPIs allowed them to create a standardized execution plan for opening new offices, which greatly increased the speed and reduced the associated cost. In the first 18 months after adopting Rhythm, they were able to open 15 more offices with significantly less hassle and stress and are increasing their pace quarter by quarter. "Working on company, group, and individual priorities that are all connected to the company's strategy, with different people collaborating on each other's priorities—all of this represents an ideal example of working as a team toward a common goal," explained Igor.

Quarter by quarter, Infobip's leadership team worked on executing the Rhythm playbook and was able to increase their discipline and improve their execution to bring more predictability to their progress. And the results have been amazing. They now have 50 offices around the world; they've increased staff by only 16 percent, dramatically improving their return on payroll; and they are moving quickly toward their Big Hairy Audacious Goal (BHAG)[1].

If you feel your team is hitting a ceiling caused by growth chaos, if you're struggling to achieve your growth goals or accomplish more of your initiatives, or if your growth has you feeling out of control, you are not alone. Challenges like these happen to most companies, especially midmarket companies that have grown quickly over the years. They outgrow their early habits of success and begin having trouble achieving results in a consistent and predictable way. The result can be unnecessary drama, reactionary decision-making, and missed targets. If this sounds familiar, you may be missing the right execution rhythms—the rhythms that will help you achieve more of the right strategic initiatives and provide you with predictable results.

Throughout this book, we'll share revealing, inspiring, and

---

1   BHAG is a registered trademark of Jim Collins and Jerry Porras.

insightful stories from real leaders like those at Infobip—leaders like you at companies like yours that successfully developed critical execution discipline. We researched the top growth problems midmarket companies regularly face and asked leaders who have successfully navigated them with exceptional results to share their behind-the-scenes stories, openly and honestly.

Our goal is to help you develop the leadership muscles you need to make strategic course corrections quickly, achieve more of your difficult goals, and accomplish important things together as a team. When you can do that, predictability follows. The key is building a reliable execution engine that generates visibility, accountability, and consistency. You can achieve all of this without the typical drama we think of as "normal" in most companies. Along the way, you'll become a more effective leader, build a great company with an engaging culture, and spend more time problem-solving and innovating, and less time worrying about whether or not you're going to achieve your goals. By sharing the stories of how great leaders and teams have pushed through for amazing success, we'll inspire you to push yourself and your team to improve your execution rhythms and apply them with discipline to achieve predictable results!

Why Midmarket Companies Struggle—and How to Break Through

Growth challenges come in all shapes and sizes. Some companies hit growth plateaus, with revenue leveling off—or worse, dropping—forcing leaders into a reactive position. Some companies face skyrocketing revenue, creating chaos and leaving leaders feeling like they're being dragged behind a runaway train. Sometimes revenue is strong, but profitability is shrinking. Sometimes both are strong, but you see something on the horizon that could change all that if you don't act soon.

All companies face growth challenges, but midmarket companies have a faster rate of change, causing them to hit new ceilings of complexity year after year. Even though they might be adding fewer employees than large firms, they may be adding a higher percentage of new employees, with additional new layers of management. Their focus on speed often causes their new business units or divisions to become unintentionally siloed. The stakes are higher; strategic investments used to come with $100,000 of risk, and now they come with $1 million or more of risk. They face the new fear of possible market saturation or commoditization with their core product or service. They may need to find the next growth curve, which may not be a skill the leaders possess yet. And to top it off, they may now have investors who want results in a predictable and consistent way. Sometimes, success is an elixir that the leaders get drunk on. Strong growth can impair their ability to see the signs that a challenge is lurking around the next corner, and they aren't prepared to meet it. What is almost always true is that these companies have outgrown their processes and management operations, because what worked at a few million in revenue might not work at tens or hundreds of millions in revenue.

In our work at Rhythm Systems, where we've helped companies execute more than 3,000 plans for growth over the past ten years and solved both common and uncommon challenges along the way, we have learned that most problems and opportunities fall into four categories:

→ **Employees.** Are your employees engaged, productive, delivering results, and excited about the future? According to Gallup, 70 percent of employees are not engaged. Are your employees some of the rare 30 percenters?

→ **Customers.** Do your customers love, appreciate, and refer you? If you don't understand them deeply and aren't connecting with their critical needs, they may not—you may struggle to keep or attract the best, most profitable customers.

→ **Processes.** Do you have healthy operations and processes that you can scale for the future? Without a commitment to continuously review and improve your critical processes, you might struggle to scale as your sales grow.

→ **Revenue.** Do you have the right products and services, as well as the right marketing and sales strategies, to support your revenue goals, now and in the future? To answer yes, you need to feel confident in your ability to differentiate yourself with customers as they change, proactively respond to market changes, and innovate appropriately.

If you're facing problems in any of these areas, there may be a gap between your current execution and the more disciplined execution you need to achieve your goals. Studies on execution show it is the Achilles' heel of most leaders and companies. Just a couple of years ago, researchers at PricewaterhouseCooper, one of the top strategy consulting firms in the world, surveyed more than 700 executives and asked them about the capabilities of their companies' top leaders. Were they good at strategy? Were they good at execution? The results, shared in *Harvard Business Review*, were depressing: "Only 16% of top leaders were rated very effective at either strategy or execution. Only 8% were very effective at both."[2] Fewer than half the leaders studied had the confidence of their teams in two of the most critical skills of

---

2 Paul Leinwand, Cesare Mainardi, and Art Kleiner, "Only 8% of Leaders Are Good at Both Strategy and Execution," *Harvard Business Review*, December 30, 2015, https://hbr.org/2015/12/only-8-of-leaders-are-good-at-both-strategy-and-execution.

any leader and two of the most essential dimensions of any company's performance.

With the right rhythms—a Think Rhythm, a Plan Rhythm, and a Do Rhythm—you can overcome the complexity and expand your capacity by bringing focus, alignment, and accountability to your teams.

3 Execution Rhythms for Growth

→ **Think Rhythm.** Consistent, productive strategic thinking to create focus for the future growth of your business.

→ **Plan Rhythm.** Consistent, productive, inclusive execution planning to align teams' and employees' work with the company plan.

→ **Do Rhythm.** Weekly attention on doing the right work to build accountability and keep the plan on track.

Real Stories from Real Companies Just Like Yours

This book is structured as a series of case studies, because the best knowledge comes from people who have successfully done what you are trying to do. Each chapter offers a behind-the-scenes tour of a company like yours and the process the leaders followed to identify the right market opportunities, focus and engage employees in executing the company's plan, develop the operating and leadership systems they needed to scale, and so much more. The companies are diverse—from $30 million to more than $1 billion, from health care to manufacturing to retail to IT, from regional to national to global—but how they solved their problems isn't unique to their industry, their size, or their business model. Each chapter is written by a Rhythm consultant who guided that company along a path of progress. The authors will share insights and observations that will help you translate one company's experience into knowledge you can use in your own company.

You can read from beginning to end to absorb all the knowledge and experience shared, or you can start with the chapter that best addresses a problem you're struggling with right now. If you are unfamiliar with the Rhythm approach, you should begin by reading Chapter 1, which lays out the essentials of the Think, Plan, Do Rhythms to help your team get focused, aligned, and accountable. If you enjoy Chapter 1 and want more detailed how-to advice on how to implement the Rhythms in your organization, you might pick up *Rhythm: How to Achieve Breakthrough Execution and Accelerate Growth*. Or go to our website PredictableResults.com to access resources specially provided for readers of this book (use the access code R123PR). In each chapter, we'll direct you to specific online resources—guides or tools—that can set you on your own personalized path of progress.

Regardless of your path of progress through this book, we know that the Rhythm approach can give you low-drama, consistent execution that will allow you to make breakthroughs and achieve your goals quarter after quarter, year after year. We hope this book helps you fast achieve the results you desire and the goals you have set.

CHAPTER 1

THINK, PLAN, DO: A SIMPLE SYSTEM TO ACCELERATE GROWTH

Solve problems faster, reduce stress significantly, and grow more predictably

Patrick Thean

In the world of fitness, there is one rule: if you want to get stronger, you have to do more reps. It's a pretty simple rule, but that doesn't make it *easy*, does it? It's hard to make time to go to the gym. It's hard to learn how to use the equipment. It's hard to overcome those feelings of intimidation or fear of looking foolish. And yet, if we committed to show up and try every day, we would get stronger. Better yet, doing more reps would become a routine habit.

Improving your execution is just like building a muscle. It's a process and it takes regular effort. When you and your team show up and try every day, you get better every day. All the leaders profiled in this book are great examples. They are making decisions daily to do that hard work, to build muscles that will enable them to grow great companies, achieve their dreams, and give their employees a great future.

It can help to have a playbook to help you understand how to use your precious time and resources for the best results, just as you rely on a trainer in the gym—or even on the TV. That is what the Think, Plan, Do Rhythms are: a straightforward playbook or method to help you get the results you want efficiently, effectively, and predictably.

It has been said that the difference between a dream and a vision is a plan of attack. That might be true. I would add that the difference between a vision and achievement of that vision is an execution-ready plan. Success happens when a company can do this repeatedly and consistently. This is why every company needs a disciplined rhythm for consistently spending time as a team on

→ strategic thinking,

→ execution planning,

→ doing the work.

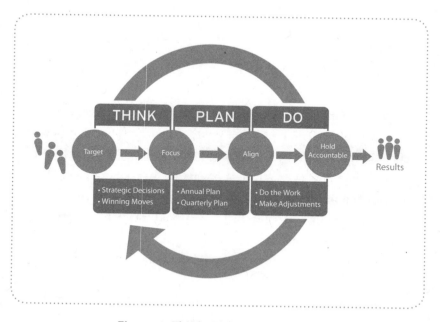

Figure 1. Think, Plan, Do Rhythms

These rhythms are necessary to move the company forward week by week. When you do them consistently, it doesn't matter what types of problems or opportunities you face. What matters is that you have a way to identify the problems, take advantage of the opportunities, and avoid the growth ceilings that kill other companies.

If you've read the book *Rhythm*, this chapter is a good, quick refresher. Or you can choose to skip over this content and go straight to the next chapter, or whichever chapter you think best addresses your most urgent problem. If you haven't read *Rhythm*, the following pages offer a quick summary of the Think Rhythm, the Plan Rhythm, and the Do Rhythm—the three elements necessary for consistent execution and predictable results. If you connect with these concepts and are looking for a guide to implementing these rhythms in your company, you should consider reading *Rhythm*.

Think Rhythm

The Think Rhythm is about getting into a regular cadence of working on the future of your business. It offers three benefits. First, it helps you strengthen your foundation for future growth. Second, it ensures that you have a continuous supply of Winning Moves—purposeful strategies for growth to double your revenue in three to five years. Third, it helps your teams focus on what to do annually, quarterly, and weekly to advance your Winning Moves.

Your Think Rhythm should include time spent working on your core values, purpose, ten-year goals, core customer, brand promise, and your three-year growth plans. The mistake that many people make is to think that this critical work can be accomplished by meeting in a room for a couple of days once a year. But it is not that easy. It is not an event. The most successful companies figure out their strategic plans one bite at a time. A Think Rhythm creates a cadence for getting this done over time and continuing to update your plans as your environment, market, company, and customers change. You are never done tackling new opportunities or overcoming new challenges.

Develop a Think Rhythm that puts strategic thinking in your flight path every *week*, every *quarter*, and every *year*:

→ Identify aspects of your core business that could be tightened to ensure sustainable growth.

→ Choose and work on the right Winning Moves.

→ Understand the opportunity costs of losing moves that steal your energy, time, and resources. Then get rid of those moves!

Plan Rhythm

The Plan Rhythm is about annual and quarterly execution planning that helps teams and individuals understand what they are supposed to do every quarter and every week to achieve the company's plan. It brings focus and alignment to everybody's work. Every year and every quarter, you have an opportunity to create a vision that energizes your teams to achieve a goal. And if you back up the vision with realistic execution plans, metrics, and tracking tools, everyone will know how they're progressing and if they need to make adjustments.

Think of each quarter as a 13-week race to achieve your goals. If that is going to happen, it is critical to have clarity, focus, and alignment with your team. Here is how the Plan Rhythm provides you with the winning formula to succeed every 13 weeks:

→ The Plan Rhythm begins with decisions about company priorities that will drive your strategy forward, making sure that every single leader understands and is aligned with those priorities.

→ You then cascade the plan to the various departments and teams in your firm, creating priorities for teams and individuals. This allows everyone to understand *and agree on* what they need to achieve as individuals, as a team, and as a company.

Begin with the end in mind by discussing and agreeing on what success looks like for each and every priority. We teach and believe in this Red-Yellow-Green process:

→ **Green:** This is the goal. This is how you describe success.

→ **Red:** This is failure or unacceptable performance. If the goal or key performance indicator (KPI) comes in red at the end of the quarter, you have failed as a team on this goal.

→ **Yellow:** Between Red and Green. While you have fallen short of your goal, you are at least performing above the failure point.

→ **SuperGreen:** This is the stretch goal!

Complete your execution plan with the right few KPIs and dashboards. You will need a balance of results indicators (like revenue or profit) and leading indicators. Leading indicators are KPIs that can give you some insight into what is about to happen with a result indicator. They are future focused and predictive. They help you peer around the corner. Accountability to the right leading indicators with clear success criteria will drive performance on your most important priorities and goals, week by week.

Planning your quarter every quarter with these tools will set you up to achieve strong results each and every quarter.

Do Rhythm

The Do Rhythm is about accomplishing your execution plan. It's about running the best 13-week race you can as an individual, department, and company. Using the priorities, KPIs, and dashboards you created as part of your Plan Rhythm, coupled with the weekly Do Rhythm, you will keep your teams focused, aligned, and accountable for achieving your quarterly plan.

The Do Rhythm consists of a series of meetings and activities designed to help you get work done, make decisions, and move your plan forward faster:

→ **Meeting with Myself.** Prepare to have a great and productive week. Spend thirty minutes each week reviewing the week that just ended along with your priorities and KPIs, setting your priorities for the coming week, and identifying obstacles that might keep you from achieving your goals for the week or the quarter. Every team member should do this as part of their personal preparation, which will enable them to contribute their best when the team comes together weekly. Be prepared to discuss any insights and solutions at your Weekly Adjustment Meeting.

→ **Weekly Adjustment Meeting.** Meet with your team to realign and focus on achieving the plan for the quarter. This is not a status meeting. It is a working meeting, to proactively discover what opportunities you can take advantage of or any obstacles that might be lurking to sabotage your success for the quarter.

→ **Adjustment Meeting.** Meet with the right team members to focus on and solve a specific problem that has you stuck. CEOs that I have interviewed are often surprised when they hear that their teams did not jump on a critical issue when it surfaced. "Why did they wait until the monthly update meeting to bring up the issue?" Instead, educate your team that they should take action by calling for an Adjustment Meeting to start working on resolving a critical issue immediately.

The only way to have a great year is to have four great quarters, one quarter at a time. And the only way to have a great quarter is to have 13 great weeks, one week at a time! This Do Rhythm helps you build a consistent habit of working with your team to have a great week, every week.

· · ·

As you read through the chapters in this book—whether you start with the next one or the one that will help you address an immediate challenge in your company—you'll learn how different companies have worked steadily to build and improve their Think, Plan, Do Rhythms in a way that helps them overcome one growth challenge after another. Just like building muscles. The most important thing, though, is that *you* take the first step. When you do, you'll discover how leveraging these rhythms can help you overcome those challenges, too, and generate predictable success for your team and your company.

For more information and tools to help you implement the Think, Plan, Do Rhythms in your company, visit PredictableResults.com.

CHAPTER 2

WIN NEW CUSTOMERS AND SELL MORE TO THE ONES YOU LOVE

How clarifying the core customer brought about a Winning Move that led to 400 percent growth in three years

Patrick Thean
with Tiffany Chepul

When I first met Dr. Stephen C. Vogt, he and his team were doing a lot of things right. At BioPlus Specialty Pharmacy, they have an inspiring purpose to do more than just dispense medication for hepatitis C and other complicated conditions or illnesses. They are committed to helping patients adhere to their often expensive and difficult therapies—treatments that last for months and often require patients to inject themselves at home. These treatments frequently come with unpleasant side effects. A missed dose could ruin the chances of a cure or even survival. Their commitment to preventing that from happening was so strong, they once chartered a private jet and a courier to deliver medication to a stranded woman in New Jersey in the days after Hurricane Sandy. Dr. V, as he is known to those who work with him, is great at inspiring his team.

BioPlus also had many strong execution rhythms in place—annual planning, quarterly planning, weekly meetings, and daily huddles. "We *are* doing a lot of things right," Dr. V said, "but I want to be better. I want to be prepared for things we may not be prepared for." He believed his team needed to up their already impressive game to respond well to changes on the horizon. They held a strong position in their industry, but he wanted them to be number one.

At their annual planning session in the fall of 2012, I noticed that they did not fully understand and appreciate their core customer. This is the primary person they serve. Many midmarket companies have only a surface or "demographic" understanding of their core customer, describing their core customers in a generic fashion based on age, education level, or market segments. It sounds like "female, with a college degree, between thirty and fifty years of age." Dr. V and his team did essentially the same thing. This is a very common mistake, a pitfall most companies fall into. So I asked them to work hard on identifying their core customer. I wanted them to be able to focus on a single primary customer and identify the person's greatest need that they could solve—and in so doing, differentiate themselves from their competition. "Dr. V, I want you and your team to ask yourselves, 'Who's our *who*?' And you only need one who. If you can do this, you can focus on this person's greatest need to create offerings that are irresistible. Don't worry about chasing anybody else. Just focus on this person as your core customer."

Less than four months later, although they were well over the $100 million mark, their stellar growth began to slow. Their goal had always been to grow at a minimum of twice the rate of the market, and that just wasn't happening. Worse, they weren't on track to *make* it happen. They needed a Winning Move that would appeal strongly to their core customer and put them on a new track of growth.

Working on clarifying their core customer and discovering how to satisfy this customer's greatest need could not have come at a better time. They needed clarity and commitment to their core customer as the strong foundation to develop Winning Moves for growth. If you do not clearly understand who your core customer is and what is their greatest need, your Winning Moves will not be as focused and powerful as they need to be. Once you can answer the question, "Who's my who?" you can work on creating Winning Moves that matter using the clarity you have on your core customer's greatest need. Without that clarity, it is easy to water down your Winning Moves to make them easier to deliver and miss the mark of delivering something great and different that your core customer will want above what your competitors are delivering. Competitors fighting for mindshare and market share are given an opening—and they'll do what they can to move in.

All the simple moves have already been made. Only the intensely difficult ones are left for the bold to capitalize on. Here is how Dr. V and his team did it and grew their revenues by 400 percent over the next three years!

How Well Do You Know Your Core Customer?

Dr. V and his executive team sat around the table in the meeting room at the Hilton in Orlando, looking concerned. I was pushing them to face the reality that they needed to understand their core customer better if they wanted their key strategies, or Winning Moves, to be successful. When you have a deep understanding of your core customer and their critical needs, you can develop and execute Winning Moves that 2X, 3X, or even 5X your business, regardless of the economic, regulatory, or competitive environment you face. "If you want to win and do something really special, you need to figure out how to

When you have a deep understanding of your core customer and their critical needs, you can develop and execute Winning Moves that 2X, 3X, or even 5X your business, regardless of the economic, regulatory, or competitive environment you face.

sell your what to your who," I said, "but you have to start with your who. If you do this, your company will be focused on the right things to help you to grow." As they spent time during that meeting thinking deeply about their core customer, they came to the realization I thought they might—they did not know their core customer as well as they thought they did.

I was describing ideas that Robert Bloom had shared with leaders in his book *The Inside Advantage.* "You must think of your customer or potential customer in the singular—as one living and breathing person," he writes. "That person you can get to know, and you can develop a close relationship with him or her. Knowing your customer—fully understanding his or her needs, preferences, and prejudices—is vital to creating a robust and effective growth strategy for your business. Quite simply, you'll have a much better chance of selling your product or service to someone you know and understand."[3]

BioPlus sold limited distribution specialty medications. Pharmaceutical companies often only partnered with a handful of specialty pharmacies to distribute those medications, because they are expensive, are used to treat rare or complex conditions, and often require special handling and patient engagement. BioPlus's focus on helping patients stick with their therapies had been a big help in growing their market share, but they needed to do more. What did that look like? They weren't sure, because their core customer wasn't clear in their minds.

At first, they thought they had four core customers: the physician who refers patients to them, the payer (insurance companies, Medicare, Medicaid, etc.) who pays for the treatment, the pharmaceutical company that supplies the specialized medication, and of course, the

---

3   Robert Bloom and Dave Conti, *The Inside Advantage: The Strategy That Unlocks the Hidden Growth in Your Business* (New York: McGraw-Hill, 2008), 16.

patient who takes the medication. Because they weren't focused on a single core customer and didn't understand who they were servicing, they had trouble developing a growth strategy that worked.

This is not a question that can be answered in a single planning session. I suggested that Dr. V get into a weekly or monthly rhythm of working with his team on an answer. It is important to commit to a rhythm of coming together with the team to solve this and other strategic problems; otherwise, before you know it, another year will have passed and your strategy will be weaker. Here is the difference between Dr. V and many other CEOs: he took action! He set up a *regular* Think Rhythm to spend time on this question with his team. His team met every week to work on answering this question. He asked, "Who is our who?" over and over. He was obsessed! They *had* to find the answer. They looked at their business model. They tracked the flow of money. They considered where they had been successful in the past.

They didn't spend a week on this, or a month. They spent *four months* coming back to this question again and again, week after week during their think time, testing their assumptions and digging deeper to find the best answer. Eventually, they felt they had it. They had to have two divisions, retail and commercial, because each had a separate core customer with very different needs. For this story, I'm going to focus on their retail customer. Their answer to the nagging question was "the person who refers and influences the specialty pharmacy prescriptions of many qualified patients."

This was the definition of the person who had the biggest potential impact on their business. It could be a clinic or hospital administrator or a pharmaceutical rep in the field, but most often it was a physician who specialized in treating a certain disease, like hepatitis C. They weren't the payer, and they weren't the person who would take the medication, but they were the influencers and decision-makers who were the source of patients and therefore the source of revenue.

That definition brought great clarity and focus to the team, but it was really just the first step.

PATH OF PROGRESS: DISCOVERING WHO YOUR CORE CUSTOMER IS

- STEP 1: Develop a Think Rhythm to work on your core customer.
- STEP 2: Gather and analyze data about your customers. Who's most profitable? Who does your team like to work with? Interview your best customers. Ask them about their unmet, critical needs. Look for patterns in the data.
- STEP 3: Write your core customer statement; describe the person (not the market segment) in 20 words or fewer.
- STEP 4: Identify any secondary decision-makers. Is there someone else involved in the purchase decision or who must be satisfied with the product?
- STEP 5: Use what you learn about your primary and secondary core customers to focus your sales, product, marketing, and delivery teams on the right customers and their needs to help you drive revenue.

Learning What Your Core Customer Really Cares About

BioPlus's promise had always been that they would create a care plan that would get the patient to the finish line with the therapy, because that would create the best outcomes. And the outcomes of their patients were better than with any other specialty pharmacy because of that focus on therapy management. When Dr. V went to their best retail customers (based on the new core customer definition), they told him about their successful outcomes again and again, and he felt so proud.

But again and again, they said something that no business leader ever wants to hear: "The patient outcomes are great . . . *but* you are so hard to work with."

They complained about how many calls they had to make for every patient they referred, how much paperwork they had to fill out, and how difficult it seemed to get patients onboard. He knew they weren't wrong. Ease of use is an overriding problem in the health care industry, but it's an essential part of customer experience design in any industry. The Temkin Group recently asked leaders at 252 companies with at least $100 million in revenue how good they were at designing the customer's experience. Fifty-six percent said they were mediocre or poor at designing for ease of use.[4]

"I went back to the team and told them what I was hearing," Dr. V recalled. The team didn't deny the feedback or fight it. Instead, they spent more think time on it.

The team knew that they had to be the best at one thing. They decided that they would become the best in the world at onboarding a patient. "There is not a doctor's office in the country that is built to withstand all the administrative overhead required to success-fully navigate the barriers to getting a patient started on a specialty medication," Dr. Elvin Montanez, senior vice president at the time (now COO), said recently. "Physicians and other customers were tell-ing us this was the number one thing that bogged them down." These medications can be incredibly expensive, from $1,000 to $10,000 a month, and payers (health plans) legitimately put up hurdles to make sure that there are justifiable reasons for their use.

....

4   Bruce Temkin, "Epidemic of Emotionless Experience Design," April 21, 2016, https://experiencematters.wordpress.com/2016/04/21/epidemic-of-emotionless-experience-design/.

During a think session, they invited one of their sales reps, who was out in the field selling to doctors, to join them. Her feedback was, "We take too long to get somebody onboard."That sentiment lit a fire of inspiration in the team. Imagine if you've been diagnosed with a scary, even life-threatening, disease, and your doctor has told you that there is a medication that could cure you or extend your life by months or years. Would you want to wait two weeks, a week, or even a few days to hear whether your insurance company would cover it? Would you want to wait to hear from one pharmacy only to find out they couldn't be the supplier, so you had to start over again with a different pharmacy? The longer it took to find out, the longer it took for the doctor to confirm the treatment with the patient, the longer it took for the medication to ship, and the longer it took to get the first dose. "Our retail customer's number one need is time saved," said Dr. Montanez.

The BioPlus team thought they had been doing well by letting doctors' offices know in two or three days whether they could be the provider for the medication and whether the insurance plan would cover it. Most other specialty pharmacies took much longer. Instead of ignoring the feedback, they asked the questions that great companies ask: *why?* and *what if?* Why did it take them even two days? With all the electronic information at their disposal, and all their technological capabilities, why did it take them so long to get back to their who? Those days, even weeks, were incredibly stressful for patients and for the physicians who were trying to save or prolong lives.

In one pivotal meeting, somebody on the team asked, "Instead of two days, *what if* we got back to them in two hours?" Dr. Montanez recalled how they felt in that moment: "A little bit crazy." Dr. V, their inspiring CEO who had always pushed them to be the best, questioned their idea. Why not commit to a day? he asked. That would still be better than what they had been doing and what their competitors were doing. He was concerned about their reputation, and the investment and effort required to make it happen. His team pushed back.

The more they talked about the two-hour guarantee, the more they believed it could be done if they focused and really dedicated themselves to it. And the more they believed it *should* be done.

Their dedicated think time about their *who* generated a new brand promise that had the potential to transform their company—as well as an entire industry. A strong brand promise can be a phenomenal Winning Move, because it should attract more of those in your core customer pool and help you retain or grow your revenue from your current core customers. It is one of the first things a potential customer learns about you. If your brand promise isn't working hard, as part of your core strategy, to help you win more customers, you're letting it languish in the land of untapped potential. As soon as the team at BioPlus came up with the two-hour guarantee, the potential became much greater. First, though, they had to figure out how they were going to get it done.

WHY SOME COMPANIES NEVER REALLY UNDERSTAND THEIR CORE CUSTOMER

Many companies struggle to focus on and understand their core customer. Why? They're overly focused on reaching everybody. They're afraid that focusing on a core customer will mean not enough market potential. And they care too much when non-core customers don't buy. But you don't always need a huge market share to grow successfully and be profitable. You also won't necessarily find success if you design products, services, and Winning Moves based on a desire to capture everyone. Ignoring parts of the market that are not aligned with your path to success is okay; strategy is about saying no more often than it is about saying yes. You need to know your core, and create the things they need and want. Focus on them and no one else.

> ## "A LITTLE BETTER" ISN'T A VERY GOOD STRATEGY
>
> One of the mistakes we often see in strategy discussions is teams benchmarking their performance against their better competitors, and then shooting for something just marginally better. Instead of incremental improvement, look for opportunities for big-step, curve-jumping improvements in your strategy think time. You might already have an ability you can leverage to do something great in your market.

Validate, Test, and Involve Everybody in Problem-Solving

"Mayday, mayday!"

Amanda Brown, senior director of admissions, wrote this comment on a Rhythm software page in mid-December 2013. Her team had just hit a serious low in its fulfillment of the two-hour brand promise. Only 87.6 percent of referrals were processed in that time frame. It was unacceptable. It was their first Red status for any week since implementing the brand promise.

The fact that less than eight months ago her department had not even existed didn't matter. The fact that the software and many of the internal processes and systems necessary to fulfill the brand promise were new didn't matter. The fact that the number of referrals they had to handle that week was one of the highest of the year didn't matter. What mattered was the 12 percent of doctors and patients who were kept waiting, and the company's reputation for accomplishing something that none of their competitors could even consider doing.

Responding to referrals in two hours was not as easy as flipping a switch. Important things almost never are. The shift required technological innovation, company reorganization, and reevaluating many aspects of their internal systems and processes. And that was just what they had to do to get started. With the help of Tiffany Chepul, their Rhythm consultant, the BioPlus team validated and tested their assumptions about this Winning Move, and then made adjustments, quarter after quarter, to fine-tune and perfect it. It takes disciplined execution, observation, and adjustments to transform a Winning Move idea into a Winning Move that bears fruit!

For instance, all pharmacy operations are dictated by software in today's modern health care world. Doctors generate prescriptions and submit them via electronic fax or directly through their own software. These orders, or referrals, are received by the pharmacy's software, and then a person has to address them and trigger the next steps. It sounds great, but the software is often poorly designed for efficient operation by the people who use it. It often doesn't play well with other systems in partner companies, like payers. It can be difficult to customize. BioPlus had to solve some of these basic problems and invest in developing better proprietary software systems to make the two-hour response possible. Even if they decided they couldn't fulfill that two-hour guarantee, the investment would improve operations and efficiency, so it was worth it.

A change like this can't be only about technology, though. It needs people devoted to making it happen. Dr. V and Dr. Montanez created the admissions department—the first team they had ever had that was entirely focused on meeting the critical needs of the company's retail core customer and fulfilling the brand promise. They put A players who had been responsible for benefits investigation and prior authorizations, like Amanda Brown, into leadership positions. They developed a learning guide and training program so they could staff up efficiently. They worked with the technology team and Dr. Montanez to figure out what changes were needed.

They would give it a month. If they could get to 80 percent fulfillment of the two-hour plan, they would be golden; they would be able to roll it out as their new brand promise. The team created a key performance indicator (KPI)—percent delivered in two hours—and Red-Yellow-Green success criteria so that they could track how they were performing week by week in the Rhythm software. But the team leaders believed they should push for better than 80 percent. Green should be 95 percent, they argued. Still, Dr. V and Dr. Montanez were convinced that anything above 80 percent would be spectacular, so Red was anything below that mark.

In March of 2013, they began. And in the first week of April, the team had a 100 percent success rate! For the last half of the quarter, just a couple of months after changing the way they operated, they never dipped below 98.9 percent!

As planning for the third quarter began, Tiffany discussed the previous quarter with Dr. V and the leaders of the admissions department. Although their success had been fast and phenomenal, she knew they would need to maintain their keen focus on a few critical numbers and establish priorities to make the brand promise work in the long term. She reviewed the plans for the upcoming quarter and the priorities for each department, checked for alignment with the company's priorities and the annual plan, looked for redundancies and gaps, and reported back to the team so that they could adjust as necessary. They felt ready to bring the brand promise to the world.

The speed with which BioPlus executed their new Winning Move was amazing. When I asked Dr. V how that happened, he attributed it to inspiration that generates alignment. "My whole career I've tried to get health care teams to work together. From hospitals to home-care companies to specialty pharmacies, and you don't ever quite get there. It's just the nature of the health care business. But when you have a great vision, which was to be the best in the world at something, it inspires others to act. Walls came down. Silos came down.

Different departments worked together; they formed committees to figure this thing out. It had a life of its own, and everyone felt a part of it, owned it."

The harder a change is, the more vivid the inspiration needs to be to generate the energy and alignment necessary to make it happen. Dr. V made this an initiative that involved everyone in the company. The secret to speed is to make such initiatives cross functional. Success comes from being able to handle the unpredictable, and we don't know what we don't know. So inspire everyone to get involved, learn, and be excited about change initiatives. Encourage people across department lines to be helpful and find ways to contribute. Then walls or silos will come down, and unpredictable problems can be caught and overcome.

The theme of the second quarter for the entire company was "Brand Promise: Two-Hour Guarantee." The company's number one priority, which Dr. Montanez was accountable for, was completing the process changes necessary. The admissions team was involved, obviously, but so was the IT team, the billing team, the pharmacy team (which had to review and verify prescriptions), and others. Every week, Dr. Montanez's team entered their status for the KPI, and when it was Yellow, they actually paid attention. They asked questions and involved other leaders from other departments, who provided ideas and comments. As members of other teams and departments collaborated and brainstormed improvements, walls and silos came down. They made the right adjustments with help from different team members from different departments.

CRITICAL EXECUTION QUESTIONS FOR YOUR BRAND PROMISE

- Have you verified that your brand promise aligns with the critical needs of your core customer?
- What are the few key activities that fulfill your brand promise?
- What actions need to be taken to make sure those activities are possible?
- How can you measure and track your success on delivering your brand promise with one or two KPIs? And what are the realistic yet ambitious success criteria for these KPIs?
- Can you establish a brand promise guarantee that can be a Winning Move in your market?

To download the Brand Promise Tool,
go to PredictableResults.com.

Adjustments Help a Winning Move Bear Fruit

All the effort paid off. BioPlus had identified a perfect moat-building move: they were offering something their core customer desperately needed but that none of their competitors were willing to do. The success of this promise began influencing every area of the business. The sales team was hearing from people who provided referrals: "This is the best thing I've ever heard." Referrals began to climb. Potential accounts who had never worked with BioPlus or had quit working with them began sending them new patients. Pharmaceutical companies were taking notice. Dr. V was asked to come speak to their leadership teams about what they were doing. One asked if BioPlus would handle their entire portfolio of limited distribution therapies.

Payers were just as interested. They understood that more efficient systems would result in savings in the long run. Suddenly, organizations they had been trying to partner with for years were coming to them. Everybody wanted to be a part of it.

BioPlus's new Winning Move was so successful that the team believed that doctors who treat other complex conditions would love working with them. They decided to push into the oncology and hematology markets just a few months after beginning the two-hour guarantee. They were right in their assumptions. The number of referrals began to grow, and grow.

All the success put a strain on the admissions team, which often happens. Growth in revenue requires growth and improvement in every part of the business. As referrals rose at the end of the third quarter, the admissions team's KPI slipped into the Yellow. With their dashboards visible to the entire company, they were able to adjust in real time and based on what they saw on the horizon. Their steady thinking, planning, and doing rhythms had them prepared. Each week, they spent time reviewing their status and discussing potential improvements. They changed their fax intake process, they automated emails to physicians and other referral sources, and they added staff. They even helped patients pay for their medications. Soon after BioPlus announced its new brand promise, it unveiled the Pay It Forward campaign. For every referral that met the two-hour guarantee, the company would donate two dollars to an organization that provides financial support to patients in need who have high copays or deductibles. For every referral that didn't achieve the promise, they would donate ten dollars.

One of the coolest adjustments they made, though, was the all-hands-on-deck approach that was possible because of how they leveraged their technology. Dr. Montanez had computer screens mounted on the walls of every room that his team uses. Those screens show every patient who is in process (coded for privacy) and a color-coded status. Any patient with less than an hour left to fulfill the brand promise is yellow. Patients with less than 30 minutes are orange. And patients with less than 15 minutes are red. And everybody on the team who has bandwidth has the responsibility for helping any other team member with an orange or red patient.

Amanda's team pushed for higher standards over the months. In planning for the fourth quarter, they were the ones who said that Green should now be 98 percent, and anything less than 95 percent success should be considered Red—failure. Unfortunately, at the end of the quarter, that's where they were. With the success of the oncology market push, the number of referrals in the last weeks of 2013 and the first quarter of 2014 more than doubled (compared to early in the year). So they continued to adjust. They hired more people, leased new space, and continued to automate what they could. By the end of the first quarter of 2014, they were SuperGreen—greater than 98 percent success—every week. And they have generally stayed there ever since.

The BioPlus team was very diligent and disciplined in their planning and execution. Many people underestimate the importance of execution, and I have seen many great Winning Move ideas die on the vine because of it. Great execution comes in the form of a strong and repeatable rhythm of planning, doing, and observing in order to make adjustments. It relies on clear success criteria that everybody agrees to, so people know what to work on, what to adjust, and when to celebrate as they cross the threshold into Green territory. Repeating this formula, quarter after quarter, is the best path to steady progress.

In the last three years, BioPlus's brand promise has helped them grow at incredible rates, far outstripping the market growth rate. Without the KPIs and dashboards to steadily track their progress week by week, the transparency that helped them identify negative trends, and the discipline to consistently review their performance, their assumptions, and new ideas for improvements, the BioPlus team could not have executed their brand promise so fast and so well. But it all began with defining their *who*.

BioPlus's ability to execute Winning Moves to fulfill the critical needs of their *who* has helped them dominate the market and grow 150 percent every year for the last three years. More than that, it has helped them change and inspire their industry. Competitors are finally beginning to catch up with the two-hour brand promise, but BioPlus has more Winning Moves up their sleeve—because they spend time every week and every quarter thinking about how they are meeting the critical needs of their *who*. They have already taken over the incredible burden of submitting appeals when a payer denies coverage for a certain treatment. It means they have to employ a team of clinicians to build a clear, strong medical case, but 80 percent of their appeals are approved, and that makes it worth it—both in how it improves the bottom line and how it helps them achieve their vision of enriching people's lives.

The Big Ideas

→ A deep understanding of your core customer and their critical needs is essential in order to develop and execute Winning Moves that can 2X, 3X, or even 5X your business, even in tough economic, regulatory, or competitive environments.

→ Develop a Think Rhythm weekly, monthly, and quarterly to answer important foundational questions about your company proactively—such as "Who is our *who*?"—so you are ready when the market shifts. Nobody has time to stop and think in the middle of a crisis. That's the worst time to try to answer big questions.

→ Focus on developing Winning Moves to address your core customer's greatest needs.

→ Validate and test the assumptions for your Winning Moves. You need to be clear about what markers of success are related to your assumptions. How will you know if your ideas are succeeding? Track your progress, adjust, and get it right. Many companies celebrate after coming up with ideas. In fact, you should celebrate only after your idea bears the fruit that you had expected. Validate that the idea works—and works to the degree that you expected it to. The details of success lie in the execution of these ideas.

→ Executing a dramatic Winning Move requires inspiration, diligence, and discipline. Too many companies give up at the first sign of possible failure. Instead, involve the entire enterprise and make the initiative cross functional. Get everyone involved. Success comes from being able to handle the unpredictable. Confining the new idea to a single department or team won't prepare them for the unpredictable or give them the resources to solve the unpredictable.

→ When you are executing a new brand promise or a new brand promise guarantee, track your progress weekly with KPIs, dashboards, and success criteria to keep your teams focused on making the right changes happen.

→ No Winning Move is perfect in concept. Success happens through the adjustments you make month by month, quarter by quarter, based on what you learn each week.

For tools and insights to help you work on your core customer and develop a brand promise and Winning Moves that meet their critical needs, go to PredictableResults.com.

CHAPTER 3

SAYING YES TO WHAT MATTERS MOST AND NO TO EVERYTHING ELSE

How addressing changing market needs resulted in a breakthrough strategy to win more customers

Liz McBride

Tim Frank sat in the conference room with his leadership team, his frustration boiling over. They had been talking about the same issues for the past two years. "Look, we have got to get to the bottom of this!"

Inergex had hit a plateau and was stuck there.

After a tough couple of years during the recession, the professional IT services firm that worked with companies to complete big technology projects emerged with three years of excellent growth. For a while, they were doing everything right, it seemed, to capitalize on the pent-up demand in the market. But then customers began saying, "We don't like the way that service is provided," or "Your competitors are offering the same IT talent at a lower price," or "It makes more sense for us to just hire someone else."

Tim and his team recognized the warning signs and responded—by continuing to add to their services and initiatives. "We were trying to do so many things that we weren't able to be really good at one or two things that could drive our growth," Tim explained. "We had nothing to hang our hat on. How can sales be successful when they aren't sure what they should be focused on selling? Where do we market? What's the endgame?" Just telling customers that their talent was better was not enough of a differentiator anymore.

When I first met Tim and the team, I could tell that no one thing had a sense of urgency to it, so progress everywhere was slow. Pulled in too many directions, Inergex was experiencing stagnated growth. Their lack of focus was showing up in their connection with their customers, who were actually saying, "We don't need you." The team was working harder for every dollar of revenue, and for almost three years, they weren't able to break through the next revenue ceiling. In one particularly tough year, they were forced to lay off some talented people, which of course affected morale.

Tim recognized they were stuck, and the team needed a new way of thinking—a better approach—to help them get past their obstacles. He picked up a copy of *Rhythm* for each member of his team. They read it over the course of a month, discussing it each week.

"It was painful for us," Tim said. The team recognized themselves in the book's cautionary tales, not in the stories of the great, successful companies. Some leaders have a tough time moving past that thinking—knowing they aren't nailing it and feeling that they are letting the company and their teams down. Luckily, the Inergex team moved on to a more positive, proactive mindset: "We know we're better than this." And they were. They just needed a way to focus their energy and resources.

To get the most important things done, you need to be able to *prioritize* those things and *commit* to accomplishing them in a disciplined and systematic way. This is essential if you want great execution of a powerful strategy that results in growth. All it takes is a Think Rhythm and a Plan Rhythm to build agreement on and commitment to the right *few* strategies or priorities—choosing what to say yes to and what to say no to. When your Winning Moves and priorities are clear, your A players can align their work to achieve them, the company can devote the right resources to making them happen, and people and teams can be accountable in a low-stress, solution-oriented way. Together, you'll make much greater progress on the things that matter most.

To grow past their plateau, Inergex needed to build this kind of focus and alignment in their strategy and execution.

Improve Your Focus, Improve Your Execution

During their newfound Think Rhythm—time spent weekly, monthly, or quarterly on strategic thinking as a team—the Inergex team realized that despite all of their many initiatives, they had not fundamentally changed with the market or the needs of their core customers. Improving their connection to those needs with a few key strategies—not a laundry list—would help them grow with purpose. We began our work with them by looking at opportunities to double their revenue in three to five years; we call these Winning Moves. They were all driven to be the best and to carve out their future with the right moves, but they had to make choices and commit. We spent months refining their strategy until they felt confident in their plan for the future. (I even coached Tim on the work from a van with a spotty cell phone connection during a camping trip.)

After months of research, discussion, and analysis of the market and their customers, they chose two points of focus: supercharge their ServiceNow practice (ServiceNow is an IT management platform that delivers productivity tools across many areas of a business), and expand managed services to offer a broad range of IT support, onsite and off, rather than just an outsourced talent pool. These thrusts made their

When your Winning Moves and priorities are clear, your A players can align their work to achieve them, the company can devote the right resources to making them happen, and people and teams can be accountable in a low-stress, solution-oriented way.

path clear. They would have to go national (rather than stay regional). They would have to recruit differently; they had typically operated within a four-hour drive of western New York. They began looking for IT talent across the nation (and eventually around the world) that lived close to major airports so that they could serve clients almost anywhere. They would need to revamp how they organized the company. And they would absolutely have to shed offerings they had been clinging to. "Our business intelligence practice was floundering," Tim Frank told me. "But at no time were we ever comfortable with the idea of shedding that business until we had unwavering commitment to ServiceNow."

That deep, driving commitment aligned the company and helped them capture the hearts and minds of customers again. Marketing became more focused and more effective because they had just a few priorities every quarter that were tightly tied to the new Winning Moves. The support teams were less distracted, so overall customer satisfaction grew—and that pushed the company to strive for becoming a ServiceNow Gold Partner. Most important, customers began to connect with the new and improved value Inergex was offering.

In the second half of 2015, their continued focus, quarter after quarter, led them to two opportunities that would forever change the company. First, they decided to acquire TREC Global, a call center technology support company that would enable them to expand their ServiceNow offering, so Inergex would be better able to help customers with ServiceNow implementations 24/7. Second, they acquired Crossfuze, a major player in the ServiceNow space. (To keep their potential acquisitions under wraps, Inergex used the best operation names, worthy of the CIA. One was known in the company as Operation Green Coconut.) After the second acquisition, Inergex rebranded as Crossfuze to leverage the brand.

These Winning Moves required improved service offerings, new marketing, and new lead generation approaches. They required new technology, new hires, and new training. But with clear prioritization of two Winning Moves and a ton of energy directed at them, it was all doable—and the work moved the company forward in leaps and bounds.

HOW TO DRIVE FOCUS ON A FEW STRATEGIES

- **Make sure you have a compelling future vision.** It can be hard to stay focused and say no when a new potential opportunity pops up and distracts you from your current priorities. Following every bright, shiny object that pops up doesn't lend itself to focus, and not every flashy object aligns with where you want to go as a company. Creating focus is much easier when you have a future vision—for the quarter, the year, or the next three to five years—that is so compelling, you really don't want to pursue anything else. If you're struggling to stay focused, you may need to reassess your short- and long-term vision.

- **Use the BHAG test.** Your compelling future vision should include a long-range Big Hairy Audacious (and measurable) Goal. When faced with multiple opportunities and limited resources, choose the opportunities that will move you closer to your BHAG faster. Proactively eliminate threats or obstacles that could keep you from your BHAG. (Download the Opportunities & Threats Tool at PredictableResults.com to document those aspects of your strategic thinking.)

- **Focus on your Winning Moves.** Winning Moves are specific strategies to achieve your three-to-five-year growth goals. If your 10-to-20-year BHAG is to climb Mount Everest, then your Winning Moves are the specific strategies to reach your three-to-five-year base camps on that mountain. You and your team identify them by brainstorming and selecting the best long-term revenue-generating ideas for the company. Once you've identified your Winning Moves, ask which current opportunities will help you execute your Winning Moves and reach the next base camp.

- **Discuss, debate, agree.** Even after filtering with these guidelines, you may still have a lot of great ideas to choose from. Discuss, debate, and agree on the possibilities with your team, taking the time to have productive conversations that lead to better, smarter decisions. This will ensure the team is excited, committed, and confident of the success of the plan.

- **Don't accept mediocrity or vague plans.** Be as specific as possible. Gain clarity as a team on the Red-Yellow-Green success criteria for each annual initiative and quarterly priority, and determine who is accountable for making sure each initiative is consistently moving forward toward that success.

- **Know when to cut your losses.** If something is Red, ask why. If a Winning Move isn't producing the results expected, ask why. Brainstorm the barriers that need to be removed and the process(es) that need to be streamlined to expedite success, or you may need to reassess the move or initiative altogether. There are times when you want something, but a lack of forward movement indicates it's time to cut the cord so you can spend your energy elsewhere. In this case, it's best to cut your losses, replace the move with something more feasible or more aligned with your core strategy and BHAG, and *move forward*. If you're struggling with Winning Moves, download the Winning Moves Tool and Winning Moves Planner Tool at PredictableResults.com.

Get Clear on What's In or What's Out

Of course, execution of company-changing strategies is never *easy*. The Inergex team struggled to build out certain solutions. They were challenged in their efforts to rapidly grow sales in some key areas. They struggled to integrate acquisitions as fast as they wanted to. But their clarity helped them push through and overcome the challenges they faced. They continued to say yes to those things that would help them achieve priorities and make their Winning Moves a reality, and no to the distractions that could pull them off course and lead them back to that revenue plateau.

"When you don't have Winning Moves and you don't have priorities and you don't have a clear idea of what to say no to, you just work your way through horrible status meetings every week," explained Tim as he reflected on what it had been like before they developed their focus. "Now people on the team know what they need to be working on. When something comes into their field of vision, they can ask good questions about how it maps to our quarterly priorities, to our annual plan, to our Winning Moves. If it doesn't map, they know they can say no. Our people never had the ability to do that before. What do we say yes to and what do we say no to—that, to me, is what execution is really all about."

Refocusing the company on being the best at meeting a specific customer need and offering a unique service experience helped propel Inergex through the growth ceiling. Morale and energy have improved, revenue is on track to double in three years, and they are a ServiceNow Gold Partner with the best customer service rating in the world. All because they developed the discipline to focus on the few priorities that mattered, pay attention to and fix what wasn't working, and say no to everything else.

The Big Ideas

→ Focus that drives growth comes from clarity backed by commitment and discipline—at the strategic level (in the form of Winning Moves) and at the execution level (in the form of annual and quarterly priorities for the company, teams, and individuals).

→ Growth plateaus are often a result of an inability to let go of poor performing strategies that don't meet the needs of your core customer. Learning to say no to opportunities that aren't the best fit for your company or your customers is key.

→ When you can move from a multitude of initiatives to a few, you have far more energy for the most important, which will bring you closer to your long-term goals and vision and drive growth.

For tools and insights to help you develop your focus and improve your Winning Moves, go to PredictableResults.com.

CHAPTER 4

EMPOWERING TEAMS TO DRIVE INNOVATION

How empowering employees and implementing the right systems freed this company up to focus on speed, innovation, and operational excellence to gain a competitive advantage

Alan Gehringer

A few years ago, I walked out of a Hampton Inn in Westlake, Ohio, after spending the day with the executive team of EMC Precision, working on their plan for the upcoming year. Bob Graney, the COO, stopped to talk with me outside the lobby doors. "I feel like we're living the movie *Groundhog Day*," he said to me, "solving the same problems day after day."

For a manufacturing firm in a highly competitive industry, innovation was critical from a process, product, service, and business model standpoint if EMC was going to continue to compete and grow. A business such as EMC doesn't have the financial luxury of repeatedly solving the same problems. They face constant pressure to improve their speed, reduce their costs, maintain or improve quality, and innovate. But like a lot of companies, management felt like they were falling short in trying to do it all—making all the critical day-to-day decisions *and* providing innovative thinking for the future. Their *Groundhog Day* experience was a symptom of a bigger challenge: they had to find a way to run the business, maintaining their focus on efficiency and quality, while also innovating to grow their competitive advantage.

EMC, a family-owned company, has been in business since 1925, which is a pretty amazing feat. They have survived tough competition over the years, and that competition has only grown as manufacturing has moved to other countries and continents. As a quick-response precision machining company that provides high-value-added products and assemblies to a wide range of industries (industrial equipment, hydraulic/fluid power, heavy vehicle, automotive, medical devices, and many others), they can't stand still.

Manufacturing companies have a reputation for exercising a command-and-control approach to management and leadership. Jeff Ohlemacher, the CEO, understood that they would need to change this approach if they wanted to be able to effectively innovate *and* achieve their Big Hairy Audacious Goal: "The best employees in the best job they've ever had at the best place they've ever worked," measured by being on Fortune's 50 Best Small and Medium-Size Companies to Work For by 2025. Jeff is a lifelong learner and understands that employee engagement, innovation, growth, and profitability go hand in hand.

One of the biggest challenges to innovation is the myth of the lone genius and the belief that only some people are capable of it. So rather than engage employees, companies tend to shut out their ideas. It's the same challenge companies were dealing with ten years ago when four innovation experts wrote in the *Wall Street Journal*, "Most companies continue to assume that innovation comes from that individual genius, or, at best, small, sequestered teams . . . But the truth is," they revealed, "most innovations are created through networks—groups of people working in concert."[5] And as Glenn Llopis, author of *The Innovation Mentality*, writes, "Innovation is not dependent on the participation of high-ranking executives, but on any employee that is a student of the business, knows their customers and knows their specific needs."[6] Not all innovation begins as a big idea. Often it starts with incremental improvements in a process or a product. Even Apple, known for being an extremely innovative company, built its product on existing technologies and is actually more of a systems integrator that creates beautiful designs and deploys them with an elegance and simplicity like few others. Trust in employees, courage to allow them to participate and act, and making smart adjustments along the way is where innovation really begins.

Innovation demands that we develop a systems approach—consisting of the right people, the right environment, and the right structure—to support creative thinking, problem-solving, and collaboration to produce marketable results. This is how successful companies encourage and drive innovation. Groups need this organization, structure, information, and systems support to be productively innovative. The Rhythm approach to strategic thinking, execution planning, and doing the right work, along with a robust tool set, can dramatically expand the innovation capacity of your teams and improve your competitive advantage.

The leadership team at EMC discovered their unique path to innovation and operational improvement that has made a major difference in their ability to differentiate themselves in a highly competitive market. While competitors have shrunk in size or gone out of business, EMC has been able to retain their customer base, respond to

5   Rob Cross, Andrew Hargadon, Salvatore Parise, and Robert J. Thomas, "Together We Innovate," *Wall Street Journal*, September 15, 2007.

6   Glenn Llopis, "5 Ways Leaders Enable Innovation in Their Teams," *Forbes*, April 7, 2014, https://www.forbes.com/sites/glennllopis/2014/04/07/5-ways-leaders-enable-innovation-in-their-teams.

Innovation demands that we develop a systems approach—consisting of the right people, the right environment, and the right structure—to support creative thinking, problem-solving, and collaboration to produce marketable results. This is how successful companies encourage and drive innovation.

their ever more demanding needs, and grow. Their efforts have resulted in a 50 percent reduction in inventory, a 40 to 50 percent reduction in various costs of production (tools, coolant, etc.), and possibly most important, a 30 percent improvement in the efficiency and speed of new product launches. They have halted the *Groundhog Day* cycle and are solving problems steadily and efficiently while encouraging their employees to step up, take risks, make mistakes and learn from them, and do great things for EMC and their customers.

Organize Teams to Create a Culture of Innovation

For years, the narrower chain of command and division of decision-making at EMC kept all sorts of small, limiting issues from being addressed. Somebody might mention that the lighting in an area needed to be better for the detail work they were doing, but that comment and hundreds more like it would rise up until they fell on the shoulders of overburdened leaders who were pulled in too many directions. They were so busy taking care of the day-to-day operations, including the all-important revenue-generating work, they rarely had time to devote to thinking about or encouraging bigger, more innovative changes, much less incremental improvements like better lighting.

Six years ago, Jeff began considering the idea of introducing Centers of Excellence (COEs) to EMC. He had first learned about COEs from a coach who was helping them set up their initial Rhythms for strategic thinking, execution planning, and doing the work. He wasn't sure it was the right time, for a variety of reasons, but he knew that it would have a positive impact on the business and their customers if they could determine how to make the idea work for them.

COEs are common in the manufacturing industry around the globe, where they're used to test and pilot new technology, test and spread best practices, develop subject-matter expertise to support different divisions, identify and test process improvements (even in management areas), or provide resource governance. They are teams of people working together to address challenges—current or future— that company, a division, or even a single department is facing. In almost every case, the goal of the COE is to improve the competitive advantage of the company. Along the way, though, through continuous improvement, they enhance their consistency, efficiency, and speed, and even create culture change.[7] Many smaller companies tend to think of them as something that only larger companies have the resources to support—based on the idea that a COE is a group of people who operate outside of the day-to-day revenue-generating work of the company. But EMC is proving that's a myth.

"I have a fundamental philosophy that was taught to me by my grandfather," Jeff told me not long ago. "It drives a lot of what we do with our employees and our customers from an innovation point of view. It is: Wherever you go, wherever you've been, whatever you do, leave that person, leave that place, a little better than you found it. And always take the high road." To Jeff, taking the high road often means making the difficult, even scary choice when it seems like the *right* thing to do to make things better. Implementing COEs at EMC and empowering employees to drive change and innovation was one of these choices.

Each COE is a cross functional team of people. If it is tied to a particular department, it includes the department leader, several people from that department, and people outside the department who support it in some way. For instance, the COE for the Swiss mill turn machining department would include a production planner, somebody

---

7   Jill Jusko, "Centers of Excellence Help Manufacturers Stay Ahead in the Game," *IndustryWeek*, October 14, 2011, http://www.industryweek.com/ lean-six-sigma/centers-excellence-help-manufacturers-stay-ahead-game.

from customer service, possibly an engineer, somebody from mainte-nance, maybe a member of the material handling department—all of them working alongside members of the Swiss machining team. Each COE is operated by a sponsor, a facilitator, and a leader, who often is a department leader, but could be a floor leader, a supervisor, or some-body else in a leadership position. And often the facilitator and leader are the same person.

COEs are separate from departments. Department leaders and staff are responsible for the day-to-day job of getting the work done correctly, efficiently, and on time. They have their own quarterly prior-ities and key performance indicators (KPIs). They address operational problems directly: scheduling conflicts, staffing needs, delays on the floor. When any of those people take a step back to play a role on a COE, they're asking a higher-level question: "What do we need to do to make this department excellent?" When a department problem can't seem to be solved or requires a deeper look, then the COE gets involved.

So, what is the goal of each COE? When EMC began forming them about six years ago, the teams turned to Jeff for the answer, ask-ing, "What do you want?"

"It's not what I want," he told them. "This is about you. What do you want?" And that is where the possible benefits of COEs became a reality to the teams.

In his now-classic book *Drive*, Daniel Pink explains that one of the foundations of motivation is autonomy.[8] It can't be very motivating or engaging for employees to see problems and not feel empowered to fix them. And when you have a lack of engagement or motivation, you certainly don't have a highly innovative team. Of course, build-ing autonomy and empowering employees is not as.easy as flipping a

8   Daniel H. Pink, *Drive: The Surprising Truth About What Motivates Us* (New York: Penguin, 2011).

switch. You can't just tell teams, "This is your show, you run it, and you decide what needs to be addressed," and expect them to change years of learned behavior. "We had a lot of folks for whom this was very new and they were really uncomfortable. And then we bring millennials on to the teams and it's like they're thinking, 'Wow, I'm allowed to talk?' It has been a process that we've had to continually build on—giving them permission to say what they think, to say what they want to do, and to do it." That approach to handing control over to the COE teams is what makes some leaders step back—but not Jeff and his executive team.

One way they have provided guidance is through the creation of Objective Statements. In Chapter 11, Liz McBride explains how to create an Objective Statement, but it essentially has three parts: a "To" statement that describes what you're trying to accomplish, an "In a way that" statement that describes how you're going to go about it, and a "So that" statement that describes the bigger benefit you're striving for. In an article about how to avoid innovation failures, one business development director explained that teams need "guard rails" (that they develop) that help them focus their work but don't rein in creativity.[9] That's what a great Objective Statement can offer; Jeff describes it as "the innovation baseline." Objective Statements can also help teams and individuals who feel hesitant to offer up ideas to speak up by making it clear why the ideas are important to the company.

Early on, the ideas were basic, and were mostly focused on fixing all the small things that were keeping them from excellence. Things like, "Move the machines farther apart so we can walk between them rather than around them." But over the years, all those items got resolved, which made the work being done more efficient, faster,

---

9   Scott Kirsner, "The Stage Where Most Innovation Projects Fail," *Harvard Business Review,* April 11, 2017, http://www.hbr.org/2017/04/ the-stage-where-most-innovation-projects-fail.

and of higher quality—and the employees happier and more engaged. Never underestimate the impact of small improvements, for it is these achievements that help develop the culture and set the stage for bigger advancements and innovations. Individuals feel better about their work environment and the company and gain the confidence needed to step outside their comfort zone. The Objective Statements have evolved, too, to higher-level ideas for excellence.

Jeff and the team have enjoyed the benefits of being able to focus on their areas of expertise and responsibility, while the COEs just keep getting stronger and more effective. Jeff told me one of the team members, Mirinit, excuses the executive team early in meetings after they are brought up to speed, so the group can "get back to work." It always generates a good laugh when she says, "You're excused," and then Jeff smiles, gets up, and leaves the meeting. The COEs take a very serious approach to their work; they review the metrics at the start of each meeting, focus on what needs to be done to move the projects forward, and take full responsibility for doing it.

As the COEs took off and started producing results, the leaders at EMC expanded the idea. They now employ all kinds of cross functional teams. They have task forces to tackle specific challenges. They have new-product-launch teams. They form teams when they bring on a big new customer, which include people who will be processing parts for that customer, from the first step in the process all the way through to shipping the parts out the door and making sure they work exactly as they're supposed to. "When we have a new customer with a complicated product, we've learned that if we don't put that team of people together and let them figure out how to produce it, we get slow-motion disasters," Jeff explained. "So we're constantly giving them permission to weigh in and say, 'I saw this. I like this. I think we ought to do this.'"

In Jeff's mind, the COEs are how the teams make things better with every project and client, how they boost innovation with all teams throughout the company, and how the executive team takes the high road in leading EMC toward a better future. This cadence and approach to organizing teams has created a measurable payoff and drives innovation.

Predictable growth requires constant improvement and innovation, large and small. You must give people permission to make decisions, act, and fail. It is only through these failures that learning takes place and true innovation emerges. Being methodical in how you set up teams to tackle improvements and new opportunities allows you to focus the effort and energy while you're dealing with the chaos of growth.

7 ESSENTIALS FOR PROMOTING INNOVATION IN YOUR ORGANIZATION

- Organize and assemble the right teams of cross functional members—consider using the COE approach to develop the right structure and cadence.
- Make sure your culture supports and empowers team members to take action.
- Provide adequate resources that include time, money, materials, systems, and support.
- Encourage research, development, and experimentation. Allow teams to look outside the organization.
- Allow failure to occur if learning takes place and adjustments are made.
- Make sure you have a good system in place to capture all the details, so you can easily scale Bright Spots (things that are working well that might be duplicated elsewhere in the company).
- Celebrate the results to promote a culture of innovation.

A Better System to Solve Problems Faster

Organizing teams for innovation is a great start, and the EMC approach to COEs was prompting a lot of progress on bigger and bigger issues that could help their departments operate faster, more efficiently, and with higher quality output. But managing the teams—their meetings, plans, actions, and progress—wasn't fast or efficient.

They were running the meetings for the COEs manually—taking notes, creating minutes and lists of actions, and producing reports, then sending those reports around. Each report might be nine pages long, and the leaders of the COEs and any affected department had to read those reports every month, figure out what to follow up on, and so on. It was a big job and it was becoming overwhelming.

EMC had been using Rhythm software for a few years before they implemented the COEs. Like most of the clients I work with, they used it to track their progress on individual and team priorities, quarterly goals, and annual initiatives, all tied to their long-term strategy. About two and a half years ago, I ran an annual planning session for the executive team. Sam Tarantino had just joined the company as the plant manager for the Indiana location. We spent some time at the conclusion of the planning session going through Rhythm to give him an overview of the software and methodology and to help get him up to speed on how EMC used it. Sam came away with a big idea. He had been feeling the pain of the COE tracking and reporting, and he saw the solution in Rhythm. When he got back to the plant, he sat down with the facilitators or leaders of the COEs and set them up in the Rhythm software. He then had them input all their Objective Statements, meeting minutes, priorities, and actions.

When Jeff paid his next monthly visit to the plant, Sam said, "Hey, check this out." He showed Jeff a COE set up in Rhythm. "What do you think?"

Jeff was amazed and immediately shared the approach with all other COEs. "I knew it would change the effectiveness of what we were doing—like night and day. And it did." It became the new method for managing meetings, plans, and progress for all COEs and similar teams.

The "chips challenge" is a great example of how better systems have helped the COEs collaborate and solve problems faster, especially across teams and locations. In machining, chips are the small bits of scrap metal that are produced as metal products are created. The company is responsible for capturing and recycling those chips, and as the machines shift from producing one product to another, often using a different metal, all the chips must be carefully cleared out, because you can't mix chips of different metals. All this is complicated further by the other big waste product: coolant. As machines cut or grind metal, they must have a constant flow of coolant at the point of contact. The chips land in something called a chip cart, which sits below the machines, and the dirty coolant flows into a sump tank.

Managing all of this can be a big hassle and time-consuming, not to mention dangerous to the operator. At EMC, it was taking an hour to clean out the sump tanks, and the machinery can't operate while this is happening. To avoid mixing metals, the people managing those machines had to clear out chips from nooks and crannies with their hands, which even with good gloves resulted in cut and dirty fingers. It was a problem that had to be solved, and the COE for the Northrup, Ohio, Swiss mill turn machining department was determined to find the solution.

Some of the Swiss mill turn team members began by attending an industry conference, where they discovered new and improved sump suckers, which extract the coolant faster and better (think high-powered suction) from the tanks and would eliminate the need for the operator to place their hand into the chips and risk injury. At the debrief from the conference, the members said, "We'd like to buy those sump suckers." So, they added a comment visible to everyone in the Swiss mill turn machining COE at the Northrup plant and attached some documentation about a couple of the products they had seen.

The COEs use comments to create productive agendas for their meetings. If you want to spend time on a topic in the meeting, you add a comment to the upcoming meeting, which is set as a priority for the COE. During the meeting, they work through the comments. When Jeff sees a solution forming in one COE that another COE could use, he just puts a comment in that second COE's meeting priority for them to check out what's in Rhythm. He can point them to good resources without having to be overly involved in their discussions. And he's coaching the COE facilitators to start doing that for their sister COEs at other plants, so that everybody is sharing in the progress made by certain teams.

The Swiss mill turn machining COE, at their next meeting, discussed the sump sucker project and whether they had enough energy to devote to it given the other projects underway already. It would require research, testing, developing recommendations, and more. In the end, they decided to move forward with it and assigned an action for researching the products and developing a recommendation to a member of the team. This team member worked with a few others to create a video that showed how the Northrup machining department was currently managing its waste by-products, and then brought two machines in for trial runs. The COE members played around with the machines and found one they really liked. From there they put a demo together and developed a proposal that included savings in time and money and improvement in working conditions, which they presented at the executive team's Weekly Adjustment Meeting. The executive team approved the proposal and they bought the sump suckers.

The new sump suckers reduced the emptying time from an hour

to about seven minutes, and the operators didn't end up with tiny bits of sharp metal all over their hands. The improvement freed up valuable machine time to make parts for customers, rather than sitting idle during cleanup.

Soon after the project was completed at the Northrup plant, Jeff was attending the COE meeting for the Swiss mill turn machining department at the Indiana plant, where the topic of chips was on the table. He told them to pull up the priority in Rhythm for the Northrup's COE for the second quarter. There, they found a link to the video, the proposal, and the current KPIs that revealed how the new machines were improving metrics at the Northrup plant. The solution is now spreading throughout the company where appropriate. It is an example of the type of solutions the COEs are generating at a rapid pace that help reduce costs and increase speed and efficiency. All that translates into better service for customers.

Once some basic problems were solved, the team's energy could be redirected to next-level problems that required more innovative approaches. "Using Rhythm as a tool keeps everybody focused," Jeff explained. "In meetings, you can look at strategic plans, one-year plans, quarterly plans, and everything is perfectly connected. You can drill down into priorities and look at comments and open relevant attachments, and you have your dashboard open, showing you the critical priorities or KPIs for that COE. Every KPI and priority has Red-Yellow-Green success criteria, so we can always see progress and ensure we know what the goal is. It just puts so much information at the team's fingertips." It also creates accountability and a clear understanding for the team of what they want to accomplish.

That kind of clarity, communication, and focus helped the Swiss mill turn machining team move on to next tackle the problem of their chip cart. The team was hearing constant complaints about the chip cart's design and had looked on the market for something to solve their problems, but hadn't found anything. Jeff attends all the COE meetings, at least for the time being, and 99 percent of the time all he does is listen. At one meeting, they asked him, "Could we design our own cart?" He looked at the head of the department, who was also leading the COE, and said, "It's your department, what do you want to do?"

The department head responded, "Well, who should we assign the action item to?" That made everybody chuckle. One member of the team volunteered for the responsibility, and another was assigned to work with him on it. They spent months gathering data and feedback. They talked to all the stakeholders. They talked to the materials handling department, who told them that a bottom with a slight angle would help the oil (the coolant or lubricant that ends up coating all the chips) drain better and they wouldn't have to lift the carts to drain them. They changed the height of the sides to make sure the chips were better contained. They kept the team updated on their progress and presented a cart design and proposal for getting a prototype made. They tested it thoroughly, and a few months later ordered a dozen of them. They even researched the exact paint used on their machines so that the carts would match and look like a unit. "You just don't get that out of folks that aren't engaged," Jeff said. Given that Gallup's *State of the American Workplace* report for 2017 showed that employees in manufacturing are the least engaged,[10] other manufacturing companies might pay attention to what EMC is achieving.

The self-designed new chip cart inspired other teams. After a huge investment in technology and machinery being used in the plating department, the people working the machines were facing challenges with the racks that held the parts during plating. Because they couldn't find one on the market that would solve the challenges they were facing, two employees—Walt Mercer, who works in the tool room,

---

10   Gallup, *State of the American Workplace*, February 2017, http://www.gallup.com/services/178514/state-american-workplace.aspx.

and Tony Bailey, who works in maintenance—said during a meeting, "Give us an action item to design a new rack." The two men developed what they have named the Mercer Joint Rack. They discovered that there's a demand for adjustable racks like the kind they developed, and so they are in the process of getting a patent so they can potentially market and sell their new design.

It will be the first patent EMC ever files. For a company devoted to helping other companies produce their patented products, that's a big deal.

THE RHYTHM APPROACH TO PROBLEM-SOLVING

Use the Rhythm Breakthrough to Green Tool to identify possible solutions to your challenges or possible enhancements for your product or service.

- Identify the current state (the problem or opportunity) and the desired state (what you want to achieve).
- List and brainstorm potential causes of the problem, or limiting factors. Narrow your list down to the top three possible causes.
- Brainstorm possible resources to help fast-track learning and development.
- List potential solutions, approaches, or enhancements. Use the Rhythm Idea Board or a similar tool to help narrow this down to your top 3 possible solutions.
- Create a recommended action plan and test your solution.
- Review results and adjust as needed.

To download the Breakthrough to Green Tool, go to PredictableResults.com.

Delivering on Innovation Requires Great Execution

Regardless of how or what you innovate, you've probably faced the fundamental challenge that every company faces: how to turn ideas and plans into executed action that helps your company grow. *Ideation without execution is useless.* Unfortunately, execution—the rollout to internal clients, external clients, or both—is also the most common failure point.

According to an article in *Harvard Business Review*, 42 percent of executives responding to a survey about innovation said that the transfer from the innovation group to the business unit responsible for the full rollout needed serious work or was terrible.[11] The problems boil down to issues of whether or not the right people have a hand in shaping the project, communication, and whether or not one person is responsible for making sure the project doesn't fall through the cracks or drop to the bottom of the priority list. What the article is saying is that innovation, just like strategy, can fall apart at the point of execution. As the author of the article writes, "When a CEO announces a major initiative to foster innovation, mark your calendar. Three years later, many of these ambitious ventures all have quietly expired." I've read almost the same words about any big strategic initiative. That is why it is so important to organize your teams the right way and create a cadence to do the work with a system that helps you execute effectively to drive real results.

The EMC approach to driving innovation also helps overcome this common failure point, because they have such dedication to

---

11   Scott Kirsner, "The Stage Where Most Innovation Projects Fail," *Harvard Business Review*, April 11, 2017, http://www.hbr.org/2017/04/the-stage-where-most-innovation-projects-fail.

execution planning and doing the hard work of full implementation. It is essential to how the company operates in all areas, from the executive team to the factory floor. Every year, the executive team takes two to three days to discuss their strategic initiatives and Winning Moves and then plan their year. Every quarter they take two days to develop execution plans for a handful of priorities for the company and each department that support progress toward their annual goals. They follow this same approach for the COEs, carefully establishing focused priorities and actions to provide enough energy to see each priority, each project, all the way to the very end, successfully.

As EMC saw the successes of COEs mounting, they decided to implement the cross functional team approach to help tackle a different challenge: bringing on new clients or projects. It began when they were considering a new client with a product unlike anything they had ever made: the TenPoint crossbow. It would also be the first time they would launch a new customer while also innovating their internal processes to serve the needs of that customer. Without careful planning, collaboration, communication, and the right problem-solving team, it could be risky.

They began by assessing the opportunity and asking the people who would have to accomplish the work, "Are we ready to take on this project?" The sales and leadership team laid out all the facts, and the cross functional team developed priorities and actions for researching the opportunity and developing recommendations. They went away for a week and explored the design, the specifications, and everything that would be involved. And then they came back with a thumbs-up.

The leaders formalized the TenPoint crossbow team and then sent the members and others responsible for making the parts to visit the client, to learn more about the product, its needs, past challenges, and future goals, so that they could effectively plan their execution to surpass the client's expectations. The team approach expanded their ability to solve problems and make the best decision for the company and for the client.

Three years later, that team is still in place, continuously improving the machining process they developed to serve the customer and the product they're delivering. Other new client or product teams have been formed and then dissolved once that project was running as smoothly and efficiently as they could get it.

"Occasionally, we'll have a new client or product come in that is highly aligned with how we work and our areas of greatest experience, and we'll think, 'We don't need a COE for this one. It's straightforward.' Guess what happens? We are reminded again of the important role COEs play."

The excellent execution planning at EMC not only helps them innovate their own offerings, it allows them to support their customers' innovations. One of the company's competitive arenas is new product launches: they help clients through the difficult initial stages of designing and planning the manufacturing of the critical parts they need to successfully launch their products on time. EMC's approach to steady, predictable execution allows them to bring great ideas to fruition. They also have the core competency of being extremely responsive and delivering very quickly to meet their customers' needs.

"Over and over again, we've seen resources and time wasted on initiatives that die on the vine," wrote Alessandro Di Fiore, the founder and CEO of the European Centre for Strategic Innovation, and one of his colleagues last year.[12] The topic was the challenges of B2B collaborative innovation. One key to success, they explained, is the need for good planning, a process for carefully selecting ideas to pursue, and "sound decisions

----

12   Alessandro Di Fiore and Jonas Vetter, "Why B2B Companies
     Struggle with Collaborative Innovation," *Harvard Business
     Review*, March 16, 2016, http://www.hbr.org/2016/03/
     why-b2b-companies-struggle-with-collaborative-innovation.

about resource allocation and governance." EMC has found a management approach to innovation that incorporates all those pieces and more. They continue to use Rhythm to find ways to be faster and more transparent, and to improve communication and collaboration.

• • •

With every problem solved, EMC has improved their competitive position a bit more. Today, they are a company to turn to when you have an urgent need for fast speed to delivery, when you're rolling out a new product and want to make sure it goes smoothly, or when you need flexibility paired with exceptionally reliable quality. They are constantly looking for new ways to raise the bar of excellence for service and processes, and they have the right systems in place to make that effort a success.

EMC has a very bright future in front of them, one that I believe will span even more generations, putting them in a very elite group of companies. With their cost savings from their continued innovation and improvements, they've been able to invest in a new semiautomated chrome plating line, the latest technology in Swiss machining and horizontal machining, and robotics, which enables them to serve their customers faster and with more product offerings while improving the work environment for employees. They even had the honor of a presidential visit when President Barack Obama was on a tour through Ohio in 2010.

They have achieved a lot by implementing COEs and the right systems throughout the company. What is learned in one COE is available and used throughout the company to help other COEs accomplish their goals and continue making EMC a world-class company. Their approach has also freed up leadership to focus on the future, while empowering their employees to improve and innovate. EMC is a great company that has every intention of continuing to learn, innovate, improve, and grow.

The Big Ideas

→ To retain their competitive advantage, midmarket companies must be innovative—in their processes, products, services, and business model.

→ Innovation is almost impossible in an environment where employees are disengaged or not empowered. Consider how you're organizing your teams to create the right environment, and how you're supporting those teams with effective systems.

→ To innovate, you must give employees the resources of time, money, and permission to experiment, make mistakes, learn, and make adjustments. It is through this process that true innovation occurs.

→ With the right systems, you can increase the power and speed of your problem-solving and innovation efforts. And when you do find solutions, it is much easier to spread those solutions throughout your company. Don't let yourself or your company end up in a *Groundhog Day* scenario.

→ Objective Statements provide your innovation teams with clear intentions, desired outcomes, and deliverables that drive results.

→ Ideation without execution is useless. If you want to improve the results from your innovation efforts, you must focus on improving your execution planning and weekly meeting cadence to get the right initiatives done successfully.

CHAPTER 5

ALIGNING BUSINESS UNITS AND KILLING SILOS

How a complex company negotiated shared resources, killed confusion, and accomplished more as a team

Chris Cosper

The leader of the automotive business unit at Flexfab, Kevin Church, had just presented a well-thought-out, thorough plan for the year, designed to meet the company's aggressive growth goals. It included a comprehensive list of people, technology, capital, and initiatives required to achieve the plan. It outlined a five-year forecast based on existing business, new opportunities, cutting-edge technology, and potential partnerships. It was everything Matt DeCamp, Flexfab's CEO, had asked for.

There was one small problem. Automotive was one of four business units; the other three—aerospace, rail, and heavy-duty trucks—were waiting in the wings. But Flexfab didn't have the resources to accomplish everything in *this* plan, never mind the goals or initiatives of the others. It wasn't the budget that was problematic but the fact that the company's engineering, production, and other support teams would have to quote, design, and deliver all existing and new work for the automotive clients, as well as the clients of the other business units.

Matt understood the problem they were facing. Flexfab's structure is based on a shared pool of production, technical, and support resources spread out over four continents, and increasingly those teams were bumping up against bottlenecks that had the potential to slow the growth of the company. If the leadership team was struggling to prioritize opportunities at the highest level or create alignment across the business units, how were the people trying to accomplish the work day by day supposed to?

When we met Matt later that year, he had already been the CEO of Flexfab for twelve years and had led the company to more than double its revenue in the prior seven. They had expanded their reach into new markets for silicone and composite parts to move air and fluids through engines. (More than likely, you've owned a car and have flown in a plane that runs with their parts.) When his father, Doug, was still CEO, Matt served as a business unit leader. He knows firsthand the pressure the leaders are under to deliver plans that show strong support for growth. But he was also hearing from other leaders in the company that their teams were overwhelmed with work and their resources stretched too thin. When a high-priority project for one business unit and a high-priority project for another launched in the same week, what were they supposed to do?

Flexfab had evolved through several different business structures over the years in an attempt to maximize resources and still maintain a strong focus on meeting the needs of customers in different industries. The 55-year-old Hastings, Michigan, company was founded by Matt's father and originally focused on supplying silicone hoses to the government and aerospace industry. As the business grew, their capabilities expanded, and new opportunities presented themselves, they pushed into other industries. They adjusted their structure along the way, moving from a traditional departmental approach to a traditional business unit structure, in which each unit had their own engineering team, quality team, sales team, and so on. This structure helped them satisfy the unique and stringent requirements of industries with different standards for tolerances, lead times, quality testing, and warranties. Though their focus on the customer helped them achieve preferred provider status in one industry after another, the structure wasn't efficient; it created duplication of costs in many cases and poor economies of scale. So they moved back to a traditional departmental structure in which all engineers reported to the head of engineering, as did those in quality, production, and sales. But Matt felt they were losing their deep connection with each industry, because individuals weren't developing the kind of industry expertise necessary to become true customer champions within the company.

When we first met Matt, they were about to embark on something new, a form of matrix management. They created business units that were industry specific and sales driven, but kept the rest of the company organized by functional discipline. The plan was to have specific employees in each discipline also serve on cross functional teams dedicated to the success of a particular business unit. Matt was optimistic the structure would achieve some specific goals—increase flexibility, reduce redundancies, build effective leaders, and improve the top line. Unfortunately, they still hadn't found the right method or system for aligning plans, setting priorities, effectively sharing resources, and achieving their most important goals together, collaboratively.

On any given day, automotive's most important customer and most important priority might have been competing for the same resources as aerospace's most important customer and most important priority. And each unit may have had more priorities than they could handle. Matt shared with me that it's not in their DNA to say no. "We were a very, very small company for a long time," he explained, describing the early years. "So we got business wherever we could." Their success over the years was driven by their ability to tackle difficult problems for customers, find solutions no one else could see, and deliver those solutions with high-quality standards. But not every challenge that came up required a solution that was aligned with the company's direction and strategy. It was easy to be distracted by the allure of creating new solutions, especially within a culture that thrives on innovation and collaboration with clients. "We call that overeating from the buffet of opportunity," I told him. Matt, who is personally very disciplined and health conscious, replied, "Well, we all know what happens at buffets. They're not very healthy." With four distinct business units grazing at their very own buffets, it's easy to see how the company could develop a little indigestion.

Compounding the problem, each business unit created their own five-year and annual plans, set their own priorities, and worked on their own growth initiatives. The business unit plans, combined, became the company plan. But there was little time to consider what was going on in the other business units, resulting in missed opportunities for cross unit efficiencies, sharing of expertise and solutions, or collaborative innovation internally. When you plan and operate in silos, 1 + 1 will never equal more than 2.

Matt and the team at Flexfab believed that their structure was the right approach. They just needed a way to solve these challenges before they slowed the company's progress. What they needed was an inclusive Plan Rhythm that built focus and alignment throughout the company.

Regardless of your structure, if your teams are competing for resources, if bottlenecks or silos are limiting your potential, or if the people doing the work are often confused or frustrated by a lack of clear priorities, you need to reconsider your planning process. Companies often apply a strict top-down or bottom-up approach. A planning process that begins with gathering the right information, involves the executive team in strategic thinking, and involves the people doing the work in execution planning will align the entire company, encourage collaboration on strategic goals, and build accountability to the right priorities. It can dramatically improve communication and intelligent prioritization across and within all teams. You and other leaders will have the visibility to know that the right teams are working on the right things this week and this quarter to meet the company's goals. And teams can rely on a system that drives clarity and collaboration and reduces stress. Momentum and confidence will grow throughout the organization, more of your most important initiatives will be accomplished, and you'll create a predictable pattern of success.

Move Your Strategy Off the Page and Into Action

Just before our first planning session in September 2014, Matt sent me Flexfab's existing plan (based on the One-Page Strategic Plan developed by Verne Harnish in *Mastering the Rockefeller Habits*). *Great*, I thought, *they've already worked through the big strategic questions. We can spend our time working on execution.*

When I arrived in Hastings with my colleagues Melissa Enriquez and Ted Skinner, who would be helping me get the executive team and business unit leaders up to speed on the Think and Plan Rhythms over the three days we had together, I assumed we would spend a little time validating and ratifying the existing long-term strategy. But when I pulled up the plan and looked out at the executive team and the business unit leaders, I saw more curiosity than commitment to the plan. Matt had developed this plan on his own, I quickly learned, and most people in the room had never seen it. Matt wasn't being intentionally exclusive or dictatorial in the company's strategy; that just isn't his leadership style. In sharing the plan with us prior to our planning session, he was just sharing his initial thoughts, and I had made a wrong assumption. It was an important learning moment, though. It

A planning process that begins with gathering the right information, involves the executive team in strategic thinking, and involves the people doing the work in execution planning will align the entire company.

was a clue that the default in this culture might be to work in splendid isolation when possible, and they would need guidance on how to work together to develop their core strategy, the company plan, and their execution plans. For them, it emphasized that to align the work happening in every corner of the company, they needed a core strategy that everybody understood and was committed to. Without it, planning would only get them so far.

In that first session, we needed to develop an inspiring vision of the future and a clear-eyed analysis of the company's potential, strengths, and opportunities. Having Matt's initial thoughts as a starting point was helpful. We asked the team to take off their business unit or functional hats and engage in this session as if they were an owner of the company. We wanted the specific expertise and knowledge each one possessed, but with a focus on the greater good of the organization, and without any territorial motivation. For some leaders, this shift in mindset can be a difficult part of the process. This team was eager to make the shift, though, and easily engaged in conversations about the long-term and greater good. I was happy to see it, because it boded well for the rest of the employees making a similar mental shift as we expanded the planning process outside the executive team over the coming quarters. Great execution planning begins with the ability to think about how your work or the work of your team can help move the company toward its goals.

Of course, first the company has to define its goals. So we discussed the foundational truths of the company's core business—the type of work they were passionate about, what they could be the best in the world at, and the conditions that allow the company to be profitable—and then discussed the ultimate vision for the company. What were they trying to achieve and how would they know when they achieved it? They needed a Big Hairy Audacious Goal (BHAG), a Jim Collins and Jerry Porras concept introduced in *Built to Last*. As a guiding measure of what to say yes to and what to say no to, they would strive toward a BHAG of being a "preferred supplier to each of the top five manufacturers in each of the markets they serve." That BHAG would encourage the teams at Flexfab to keep their standards high to engage the best and brightest customers in each market and make smart choices about the opportunities they pursued.

With this newfound clarity, they were able to evaluate their opportunities to grow revenue over the next three to five years through a new lens—opportunities we call Winning Moves. We discussed the revenue potential and difficulty or ease of accomplishing each Winning Move, and quickly narrowed an original list of thirty-plus opportunities to two to three for each business unit.

Turning their attention to the company plan for the year, they adopted a theme, "Prepare to grow with purpose," that acknowledged the shift from reactive growth based on immediate opportunities to more strategic and intentional growth and established priorities aligned with that theme. We wrapped up the planning session by creating an execution-ready quarterly plan for the first quarter of their fiscal year, discussing who would serve on each of the business unit's cross functional teams, and creating a plan to begin engaging those individuals in weekly meetings to discuss execution and adjustments.

Learning to Plan as a Team Is a Process, Not an Event

Setting a direction and making tough but smart choices about opportunities are essentials of effective strategic planning, and the team had made great progress by agreeing on a few long-term goals and using them as the filter to narrow their list of priorities. They had also worked well together. They're one of the most respectful teams I've worked with. Respect is one of their core values, so in retrospect it's not surprising, but I was happy to see how receptive they were to change and how much progress they made in the first session. Learning to plan well as a team while your company grows is a process, not an event. It's important to be open to necessary adjustments.

Three months later, as we were preparing for the company-level discussions, which would start on the topic of core values, I asked Matt if the business unit leaders were joining us. He told me they hadn't been invited, but would be joining the next day when we rolled Rhythm out to the business unit teams. Again, it wasn't an issue of exclusion. They were simply trying to limit the amount of time the leaders had to spend away from their day jobs, and we hadn't specifically requested they invite them again.

We went ahead and worked on core values and then developed the company plan for the quarter with the executive team. The next day, we would share the company plan and focus on the business unit plans. Not long into the second day of planning, it was clear to everybody that the business unit leaders should have been there for the first day's discussion, and it was especially clear when we had to spend time explaining everything that had been discussed the day before, over and over again for each business unit team. It might have seemed efficient for them to be involved only on day two, but it was ineffective.

The best companies learn and adjust quickly, and this is true for Flexfab. For every quarter after, and especially the next one when we worked on defining the core customer and the brand promise, the business unit leaders were involved in the company planning and thinking about the core strategy, which helped cement the broader goals they should be working toward as they developed their business unit plans. This step was possibly even more important because the newest business unit, rail, had recently won a significant contract to supply parts on one of the largest rapid transit commuter rail systems on the West Coast, and was working hard to finalize designs, manage margins, and successfully launch the program, which would require a disproportionate amount of technical resources for several quarters.

Involving all the leaders in figuring out how to make that happen was critical to their success. Together, they were able to balance internal resources, respond to the customer's needs, and successfully execute the program.

These key learning moments helped prepare the team to create a collaborative and iterative planning process that would engage the right people at the right time.

The Power of Prework to Drive the Right Decisions

Planning sessions should be about having the right discussions and coming to agreement on the best decisions. We teach this idea over and over again to avoid unproductive planning sessions that don't actually generate a strong plan for the year or the quarter. It's hard to achieve those ideals, though, if you don't know what discussions you should be having or don't have the information you need to make the best decisions. Everyone has to come prepared.

That was especially true at Flexfab, where the cross functional business unit teams held so much knowledge about successes, roadblocks, planned innovations, and market opportunities. After we worked through a few quarterly planning sessions, cascading the process to include the people on the cross functional teams (I'll describe the process in the next section), we made an adjustment toward preplanning within the teams. The goal was to capture the collective intelligence of the teams—the vital information that often doesn't make it all the way up to the executive level. In order to create the most well-informed company plan each quarter, we needed to know where each business unit stood on three key questions:

→ Are you on track to achieve your current annual plan?

→ Did you achieve your Green goal (in terms of Red-Yellow-Green success criteria) on your current quarter priorities?

→ What do you already know will require the team's energy in the upcoming quarter?

To gather this information we developed a prework packet that included specific prompts and asked the team to use at least one of their Weekly Adjustment Meetings to answer them with the team. And knowing that the business unit teams had the most insight into their groups, customers, and markets, we asked one final question:

→ Taking all the information you've gathered into consideration, what are the top two to three strategic priorities you believe your business unit team should focus on in the upcoming quarter?

The prework prepared by the teams is taken very seriously. The first day of each quarterly planning session—when we focus on the company plan, individual priorities for the executive team that support that plan, and team-level priorities for the business units—begins with a review of performance in the last quarter, and then the business unit leaders present the results of their prework so that the entire team is working with the same information. As the discussions about the company plan and possible business unit priorities continue based on a full sharing of information, the priorities might be adjusted. The goal is to agree on the few priorities that will move the company and each business unit forward. (If you want to know what happens when leaders struggle to agree on the three to five priorities that matter most, read Chapter 7.)

The magic of alignment comes from plans that are realistic, and one reality that must be addressed is the truth of limited resources. The executive team is charged with considering alternatives for allocating the company's resources in support of the most important priorities—those that are aligned with the company's long-term plans and goals, informed by the current business environment, and supportive of the needs of the departments or business units. These leaders have to make decisions about what's in and what's out of the next 13-week race. The discussion might look like a negotiation at times, or a lobbying effort, but it should always result in a plan that is fully understood and supported by all—a plan that maximizes the company's resources in a way that makes the biggest impact on the company's potential and future. The goal is to bring people together to have smart discussions and agree on the right things to work on, but ultimately, the leaders make the tough choices.

Flexfab saw this play out one quarter as a business unit leader became fiercely protective of a priority his team put forth in the pre-work they had done. His team had been pursuing a high-profile client quarter after quarter, devoting significant time, focus, and resources, and although they had not been successful in breaking through, they believed if they were given a little more time, there was still a chance they could make something happen. Had the timing been different, they may have been able to afford investing more time and energy on this, but new, more promising opportunities had risen to the top this quarter, and there was little hope that they would be any closer to landing this customer 90 days in the future. The leadership team spent quite a bit of time discussing it, driven by their passion for respecting people's ideas and insights and their desire to support a culture in which people are valued and engaged.

"They need to play it out for the next 90 days," the business unit leader told the group. "Then they'll be able to let it go."

Matt had to make the call. "No," he said. "It's time to let this one go. We can't support an unlimited number of priorities, so everything in the plan must be meaningful; we can't keep this one. I'll explain it to them."

In some cultures and with some planning approaches, that conversation might have resulted in months of disgruntlement for that team. Instead, it was a successful conversation because it was driven by the needs of the company plan, which had some new, exciting initiatives within it. They were able to let something go without feeling like they weren't heard, because the reasoning behind the decision was made very clear and they were able to see the full picture once the entire company plan was shared.

This interplay captures the truth of how you develop the best plans. The right information from the right people and clearly explained decisions build trust. It is also important to note that I have seen many more occasions where a challenged priority like this one stays in the plan because new information is shared that sways the decision. An open mind and inspiring priorities help you make tough trade-offs. And that's the strategic mindset you encourage and develop in people when you involve them in the process.

5 STEPS TO A BETTER PLAN

Every quarter and every year, you should get together with your executive team to develop quarterly and annual plans for the company, which are then cascaded down into the teams where the people doing the work will develop execution plans to achieve the company goals. Use these tips to develop better plans at every stage:

- Step 1: Understand your current environment. Do the necessary prework prior to your session to understand where you've been over the past quarter or year, what you've accomplished, what you've learned, what adjustments you made and why, and what opportunities and threats you face. This critical information will help you develop much stronger plans.

- Step 2: Review your strategy and discuss Winning Moves. Begin your planning by spending time on strategic thinking to review elements of your core strategy, discuss progress on your Winning Moves and important next steps, and share what you've learned about your assumptions and market reception. Work on the right strategic foundation for your plan.

- Step 3: Envision a great year or great quarter. For the year, do the Destination Postcard Exercise (you can find it at PredictableResults.com). For the quarter, discuss where you need to be at the end of the quarter for it to be considered a success and to stay on track with your annual plan.

- Step 4: Discuss, debate, and agree on the details.

  » Establish a main theme or focus, which is the number one thing everybody in the company should be focused on achieving. It might be a Winning Move, an aspect of your culture or core strategy, or it might even be a financial target. But it should be an inspiring rally cry.

  » Determine the measurable targets the plan must achieve and clarify success criteria for each. This can include revenue, profit, number of employees, number of new customers, new locations opened—whatever makes sense as a measure attached to your plan.

  » Identify the top three to five company-level annual initiatives and quarterly priorities, along with Red-Yellow-Green success criteria for each.

- Step 5: Cascade and communicate the plan. Involve the people who will do the work in creating an execution plan that's realistic and that has the full buy-in of everybody involved.

For more help with your annual planning session, download our *5 Steps to Creating a Winning Annual Plan* guide from PredictableResults.com.

The Moment Your Teams Actually Look Forward to Quarterly Planning

Matt turned toward me with a surprisingly big smile and a look of pride. Frankly, I was expecting relief and maybe exhaustion. We were at the end of day two of our seventh quarterly planning session and had actually finished early. The fine-tuned engineering mindset at Flexfab gravitates toward problem-solving and a deep dive into the details, but the fact that the business unit leaders got through their presentations earlier than expected wasn't what had Matt's eyes shining. "People aren't leaving," he said. "I can't believe the energy in the room."

Typically, you finish a company meeting early and people are out the door, anxious to check email, make a call, or pick up the kids. That might have been true at Flexfab a year before, but not now. Instead, many of the forty or so people on the planning teams were gathered in small groups, asking questions about what they had heard, setting up meetings to discuss next steps on a priority, or just offering a bit of advice. They had claimed ownership of the plan for the quarter and were eager to continue working together. Matt was right. The energy in the room was unmistakable. I couldn't help but think back on the large reserved group we had met a little over a year and a half before, and how much they had grown as leaders and strategic thinkers during this time. People were no longer only concerned about their individual task lists and how they could protect the time and resources they needed to get their work done. They were now concerned with the company's performance and maximizing strategic opportunities, and they were equally curious about all the business units' priorities.

A favorite saying I picked up years ago from a mentor and culture-change expert I worked with is "You are perfectly designed for the results you're getting." Your design may not be perfect, and your results may not be perfect, but they are perfectly matched. This quote was inspired by Dr. W. Edwards Deming, the famous engineer and management consultant whose breakthrough work on continuous improvement changed the way people thought about how they manage processes. Deming was also one of the first to recognize the need to break down barriers and eliminate silos. Employees need to see beyond their immediate responsibilities and think about the impact their work has on the organization as a whole.

At Flexfab, we were working to design a process that would give the team that broad view. And they were already seeing a change in their results after cascading the planning process to the teams. We were asking people to shift their perspective and think strategically about the company, their team, and their individual work, to collaborate cross functionally, and to act as champions for their business units. They understood the company's vision and strategy and had learned the Rhythm methodology of strategic thinking, execution planning, and doing the work. Implementing change and developing new habits takes time, but they were mastering it quarter by quarter.

During the first day of this particular planning session, the executive team and the business unit leaders had met to establish the company plan for the quarter and clarify the top two or three priorities for each business unit. The morning of the second day, they had presented the company plan and business unit priorities to the broader business unit cross functional teams. The business unit leaders had shared some team victories and lessons learned during the previous quarter, and then the teams had split off to build their own execution-ready plans to accomplish the priorities. (Usually, they also add one or two priorities that are more operational while working on the execution plans. I have found that if you tell a team they can have five priorities, they'll get to five every time. In my work early on with the Flexfab team, I opened Rhythm one day to review their final priorities for a quarter and just laughed. I had told them their priorities couldn't number more than five and they abided by the rule—sort of. They numbered their first five, and then listed six more without numbers. We got there eventually by creating a stronger definition of what makes a priority strategic and creating additional key performance indicators (KPIs) to track other important, ongoing aspects of the business.)

Building an execution-ready plan requires the team to address the following:

→ **Team energy:** How much energy will be required to accomplish this priority? For each company or business-unit-level priority, what are the necessary supporting priorities? Every priority in Rhythm has an energy map that shows users how many team or individual priorities support it. Within each business unit at Flexfab, they had to establish supporting priorities, owned by individuals on the team, that would make the success of the business-unit-level priority possible. A priority doesn't happen unless people are doing the necessary work to make it happen.

→ **Accountability:** Is accountability for each priority and KPI clear? Everyone on the team should be in agreement about who the primary owner is for each priority, what milestones will be met to accomplish the priority, when the priority should be completed, and how the team will measure success at the end of the quarter.

→ **Focus:** Is everybody on the team focused on the right things? Everyone's individual priorities should line up with and support the company's or business unit's priorities. And in addition, everyone should have a clear picture of what the main focus for the whole company is every quarter. What's the one main thing we want to be able to say we accomplished at the end of this quarter?

→ **Financial results:** Are we likely to have a good financial result this quarter if we successfully execute this plan? It's easy for teams to get caught up in the excitement of new initiatives and future growth, and take their eye off the critical daily work that must still happen to maintain the current business. Every quarterly plan should include financial targets and clarity around how the team will meet these targets.

Asking the teams to develop the execution plans is an important step in the process because only those expert in actually doing the work can determine the specific energy that has to be applied to accomplish the priorities and set realistic Red-Yellow-Green success criteria for them. This step generates commitment to the plans and increases the likelihood that they will be successfully executed.

Alignment Doesn't Happen Until All the Plans Are Shared

The final step in planning, and the step that helped generate the great energy Matt noticed, is to share the plans in a way that builds cross team understanding, support, and collaboration. This is a huge benefit of alignment. At the end of each planning session, the business units share their plans with the rest of the teams. People ask clarifying questions, identify and solve any potential resource constraints (when two plans are pulling too heavily from the same resource, setting up the potential for a bottleneck or failure on a priority), and identify any potential synergies between priorities that could allow them to execute faster or with fewer resources. I've seen companies try to skip this step, but the most successful companies do this and are consequently able to move much faster and eliminate wasted time and resources down the road.

While the company plan and business unit plans are finalized by the end of the two-day session, the process isn't 100 percent complete until the quarterly plans are shared with the rest of the company. Flexfab has hundreds of employees and only about 40 are directly involved in the planning process. Every individual in the company should have an understanding of where the company is going, what the plan is to get there, and what they can do right now to help. They should be inspired by the company's BHAG, confident in the company's Winning Moves, and aligned with the execution plans. This is what makes the difference between employees that lay bricks and employees that build cathedrals. Some companies pull everyone together once a quarter for a town hall–style meeting, some share the quarterly plan in a newsletter, some have a series of department or location meetings, and some depend on their leaders to share it with their direct reports.

The important thing is that everybody understands and is supporting the plans of the business units and the plan for the company. The process has even adjusted the role of the executive team. "Our sole purpose is to help remove roadblocks," Matt explained. For the executive team, a consistent quarterly priority listed in Rhythm is "business unit roadblocks." Each month, if a business unit is stuck on a priority, the leader enters it into Rhythm as a Red or Yellow status, and the team meets to discuss the challenge and how they can help break the block down. If Bill Haywood, who runs the aerospace business unit, says, "I just don't have enough technical resources to get this project completed on time," it's the executive team's responsibility to look for ways to free up resources for Bill to use. That's what alignment looks like in action.

4 TIPS FOR SUCCESSFULLY CASCADING YOUR PLAN

- Collect insights from cascade teams before you do company planning. Remember that the best information about what's going on in your company, with your customers, and in your operations lies with the people closest to the work. Gather their input in the form of prework before building the company plan.

- Build a strong plan for the company before building individual team plans. The company's focus, priorities, and targets, determined by the executive team in the company planning session, should serve as the foundation for all other team plans.

- Determine the right rhythm for cascade planning in your company. Some companies bring all of their teams together for a day, some have their teams meet independently, and some work virtually. Begin designing your system and schedule for cascade planning and then commit to improving it over time.

- Provide an opportunity for departments to share their plans with one another. Scheduling this time will give teams a chance to understand how their priorities impact other teams, discuss and solve any resource constraints before the quarter begins, and ensure everyone is aligned and working toward achieving the company's goals.

Focus, Alignment, and Accountability Will Drive Results

"In the past, you only knew what was going on in your own business unit," Matt said to me recently. "And there was a lot of stress associated with not having enough resources to get everything we had said yes to done. Now the leaders know what's going on all across the company, and we're finally able to see some of the things we've talked about for so long get done."

Focused effort, alignment, and accountability to a realistic plan have driven progress on projects and priorities. The massive commuter rail program launched successfully and profitably, as have numerous other programs since then. The teams are able to document their priorities in Rhythm software, advance them weekly, and discuss the results and next steps in quarterly planning sessions. They are getting the most important things done, and they're able to measure their progress, which helps build momentum toward future successes. Today Flexfab's business unit teams are thriving. Their discipline, communication, and collaboration are improving, and the rhythms, habits, processes, and tools they're implementing will continue to support their matrix management structure.

Matt is encouraged by the improvement in their resource requirements, too. They are becoming more efficient in everything they do and have dramatically improved their return on payroll. They are returning more than 90 percent of quote requests on time, have successfully launched and delivered numerous new products and projects, expanded their manufacturing capabilities in both quantity and quality, and have won over $100 million in new contracts over the past year—and they are doing all this today without having added additional people, boosting their return on payroll. And while there is now greater uncertainty in the global economy, US trade policies, and other macroeconomic factors, Flexfab has certainly built a strong and disciplined foundation that will allow them to weather the storm when times are tough and ride the wave when times are good.

With a clear vision of how to move closer to their BHAG, unified cross functional teams of experts who are clear about the expectations and committed to fulfilling them, and a collaborative process for planning, adjusting, and executing every day, week, and quarter, the company has been able to take on complicated new projects, make progress on priorities that had been stalled, and consistently develop new capabilities to serve existing and future markets. Their enviable growth and market domination has been driven by new levels of clarity, alignment, and collaboration. Flexfab is confident in their ability to answer the question, "What's next?"

Big Ideas

→ When you create well-informed and timely annual and quarterly plans that are realistic and strategic, you greatly increase the likelihood of successfully executing the plans, building momentum over time, and creating a new level of accountability, execution, and success.

→ A planning process that begins with gathering the right information in advance of any discussions or meetings will generate a stronger, more viable plan.

→ The executive team is charged with spending time on strategic thinking and considering alternatives for allocating the company's limited resources in support of the most important initiatives or priorities—those that are aligned with the company's long-term plans and goals, informed by the current business environment, and supportive of the needs of the departments or business units.

→ The magic of alignment comes from plans that are realistic and developed with broad participation. The more people you involve in the planning process—whether through prework, participation in the planning session, or reviewing and communicating the plan afterward—the higher the level of ownership and commitment your organization will have to achieving the plan.

→ An execution-ready plan is one that can pass four tests: Is there enough *energy* devoted to each initiative or priority, in the form of supporting priorities? Is one person *accountable* for each priority and KPI, and is it clear how you will measure success at the end of the quarter? Is everybody *focused* on the most important pieces of the company plan, contributing some of their valuable energy to it? Are you likely to have a good *financial result* for the quarter if you successfully execute the plan?

→   Finding the right planning process for your company is a journey and will require some trial and error. It's important to assess what worked well and what can be improved the next time around after you complete each quarterly planning cycle.

For help developing the right Plan Rhythm in your company, one that improves execution of your strategy, go to PredictableResults.com.

CHAPTER 6

SCALING YOUR COMPANY FOR RAPID GROWTH

*How investing in intentional leadership,
transparent operations, and a culture of collaboration
helped overcome the chaos of fast growth*

Cathy McCullough

Any CEO and executive team should be proud of growth. After all, it takes a lot of hard work, energy, and effort to grow a company. Advancing revenue and increasing profit margins is something to celebrate. Growth, though, also presents a new set of questions. How can we control the chaos of growth around here? How can we protect our best people from burnout? How can we prevent or break down silos? How can we keep up with all there is to *do*? Leaders of organizations of all sizes and sectors are asking these types of questions as they work to balance the complexity of leading the people within their companies through the maze of growth and the changes that growth requires. The leaders at Arbill were no different.

Since 1945, Arbill has been a leader in workplace safety by providing training and personal protective equipment to companies throughout the US. Their mission is to help companies control costs, engineer out safety risks, and minimize exposure to claims, all while helping every worker go home safe. They were achieving these goals, and as a result, the company was experiencing double-digit growth. But along with rapid growth came their own fair share of chaos. The chaos had been limited so far, but the executive team recognized the potential for increased frustration if they didn't prepare for continued rapid growth. As executive-level leaders know, complexity is the devil for fast-growing companies, and it can put the leadership team in pain.

There's a tipping point when it comes to growing a company, and at that point it becomes imperative for leaders to begin leading differently. This is exactly what Julie Copeland, the CEO of Arbill, recognized. While she welcomed rapid growth, it required a shift in how she and her executive team led and managed operations; otherwise, they would no longer be running the company. It would be running *them.*

The Arbill team could see growing pains headed their way. After all, new streams of customers would mean new products and more inventory. Their distribution centers would be forced to keep up with large amounts of stock flowing in and out, while those in purchasing might struggle to forecast what products would be needed in which warehouse. The accounts payable team might struggle to keep up with the influx while ensuring smooth cash flow. Julie and her team didn't want these potential struggles to engulf them. They didn't want to be working hard for minimal progress. They didn't want to just push through the encroaching pain; they wanted to avoid it or resolve it so they could continue to grow with purpose. In Julie's words, "Growth is exciting, and we'd worked hard for it! But I realized that what we were doing, in the way we were doing it, wouldn't create the kind of future we envisioned. If we didn't properly set the stage for growth, it would make existing in this space stressful. I wanted a calm business that did well and could scale." In short, Julie realized she and her team didn't need to work harder. To brace for rapid growth, they would need to work *differently*.

In my twenty years of consulting, I've seen leaders struggle with this reality—chaos caused by fast growth—because they haven't laid the proper operational and managerial foundations. It can be a sign that the engine driving revenue, quality, customer happiness, and employee engagement is about to start sputtering. And if your sales are causing internal processes to break and your teams are running around like chickens, your profit goals will suffer because of rework and waste. If you are a hypergrowth company, this chaos can result in an implosion. Sales at Arbill were going well, but the executive team recognized that their operating infrastructure and management systems could be a weak foundation for supporting continued growth.

The pain of growth, which happens when we aren't prepared for it, can be solved by building scalable operations for increasing and supporting sales, which will also improve margins, customer satisfaction, and employee happiness. But scalable operations don't start on the front lines, surprisingly. They start with a leadership team adopting a scalable management framework—one that supports visibility throughout the company, progress on key strategic initiatives, cross functional collaboration, and continuous improvement. When you have this foundation, managing change, which is what scalability is all about, becomes much easier. Instead of being victims of the complexity that comes with growth and change, your team members can be masters of low-chaos strategic execution.

Growing a company requires the conveyance of a clear message around your strategic intent. It requires systems and processes that must be built over time, and it requires building a company culture that understands the operational side of "how we do business around here." Without this common understanding, you'll spend a great deal of your time *fixing* things or situations versus *building* a business.

It was time for Julie and her leadership team to position the

Scalable operations don't start on the front lines, surprisingly. They start with a leadership team adopting a scalable management framework—one that supports visibility throughout the company, progress on key strategic initiatives, cross functional collaboration, and continuous improvement.

company to sustain incredible growth. They decided to establish healthy rhythms and habits that would guide them in creating a strong future for the company while also eliminating silos and improving transparency and communication. They recognized the need for better management processes if they wanted to prepare their operations to handle growth.

A Powerful Framework for Leading Change

Not long after we began working together, Julie shared with me that for some time she and her team had had a vision of what Arbill should look like in the long term. Julie recognized that they needed to begin to work on executing on that vision, and to do this would require an alignment in their collective thinking about how they would do this. "The vision in our heads was clear to us," Julie noted, "but what was needed was for the team to embrace *how* we were going to move toward that vision." This was especially important because Julie knew that executing on their vision would require some key strategic changes.

Understanding the vision was a huge advantage for Julie and her team. This is because scaling for growth always requires a destination. Without a defined destination, everybody has a different picture of a future course (if they even have a picture at all). We often hear stories of CEOs' strategic proficiencies. The downfall of many a failed company, however, has been attributed to its lack of vision. Tony Mayo, lecturer in organizational behavior and director of the Leadership Initiative at Harvard Business School, has done extensive research that shows the best leaders create context for their people by shaping the company's preferred future. His research also reveals that those leaders have the ability to drive the execution of current strategic endeavors that are aligned with that future. Vision separated from any sense of present context has the potential to create very inconsistent and random results. Can you grow a company without a long-term vision? Probably. But if you want the engagement of your people along the way and smooth transitions from present state to future state, then you need to lead your people *toward* something. Doing so allows work to become more purposeful and meaningful.

Growing your company means disrupting current operations and changing the way people see the company; things can't stay the same. It requires the right kind of disruptive leadership. What I appreciate about Julie's approach is her tough resolve to be appropriately disruptive and encourage her team to recognize the changes that would be necessary in order for Arbill to reach its desired future. One of Julie's strengths is that she is willing to challenge her own thinking *first*, and then gracefully challenge the thinking of those around her as a way to help them see, and then cocreate, their next steps.

Julie and the team had crafted a future state for Arbill that captured their collective aspiration to protect 1,600,000 people by 2020. Their narrative is that they envision an ultimate future in which every worker makes it home safely, every day. In time, everyone that worked at Arbill began to understand what drives the company's aspiration, which is to *save lives*—in every single thing they do. This level of safety is Arbill's passion; it's woven into their purpose. They know they have a long way to go to reach that aspiration, but they stand firm in their commitment to partner with their clients to achieve it. Leaders at Arbill from the executive level down are evolving new products and services and adjusting operations and processes to meet their vision. They also aligned their terminology with their desired future state, which is many times overlooked when leading change. For instance, they made the migration away from a sales mentality (which only supports the concept of selling products) to one that supports the Arbill vision of saving lives. To do this, Arbill's salespeople had to make a huge shift to become what the company now calls safety advisors. Arbill's safety advisors partner with their clients to customize specific plans that will drive out workplace injuries. Arbill's goal isn't to simply sell products anymore; their goal is to partner with their many customers to eliminate workplace injuries. That can't be done by simply selling products.

Julie knew that aligning her team in a way that would move them toward the company's long-term vision meant they would have to look at everything they were currently doing through a new lens. Doing things the way they'd always done them would no longer suffice if they were going to become a total safety-service provider. To that end, they began to ask a set of questions that forced them to switch off autopilot thinking. They began to ask more strategic questions, such as: Will what we're doing today really build the bridge toward our future vision? Will being a product vendor move the needle toward higher levels of workplace safety? Will it help us to evolve toward *saving lives*? If not, what will? The questions could be daunting for Arbill, but the answers led to their need to upend their business model and evolve into being a valued safety partner that offers products and consultative services and plays a safety advisor role with clients by offering products *in conjunction with* safety programs, environmental health and safety managed services, training, talent augmentation, safety audits, and more. Making this move, though, would require them to first address the management and operational foundation they were building on.

To navigate their impending journey in a way that would clearly define *how* they would begin to execute on their vision, Arbill's executive team turned to the Think, Plan, Do Rhythms and focused first on improving their execution planning process—to direct attention to strategic priorities and change initiatives every quarter.

For instance, by employing the Rhythm methodology and software, the team was able to step back and think about Winning Moves built on their value proposition of saving lives. It was exciting to guide the team through a set of questions that allowed them to think about and provide specific thoughts around the value of what they were providing to their customers (from the *customers'* point of view). One leader noted, "It was clear through the commoditization of our products that clients and prospective clients simply saw us as a vendor and not as the *valued safety partner* we wanted to be." That realization was huge. The leadership team discussed, debated, and agreed on a few Winning Moves (their three-year, larger scale, revenue-generating strategies that would continue to perpetuate their growth).

Rarely can you take big steps forward without having to change processes, systems, and technology. Change requires energy, time, devotion to implementation, and more. And large-scale organizational change is partially about changing the way people think. It's easier for people to keep working the way they always have, on the things they've always done. Without a defined and organized pathway to lead people from where they are today into the desired future, most change initiatives will have limited results. Once the Arbill team learned to align their execution with their newly defined Winning Moves, they were engaged and ready to be guided through a planning process.

The leadership team began by identifying a set of annual initiatives for improving the internal systems needed to support their Winning Moves as well as stakeholder relationships, supply-chain adaptations, operational improvements in key departments, and more. The team was then able to work from their annual initiatives to create aligned quarterly priorities. For example, one of their annual initiatives was to create operational improvements in their supply chain. This allowed them, then, to create quarterly priorities for the supply-chain team around operational excellence in the warehouse. With this as a stated quarterly priority, they created individual priorities for the director of operations and the leaders of each of the three departments within the supply-chain team (receiving, replenishment, and shipping), such as specific priorities for improving cycle count accuracy, making a process change to paperless picking, improving receiving productivity, developing leaders on each of the teams, improving the rate of on-time shipping, and specifics around what they would do to improve picking productivity. They established key performance indicators (KPIs) for returns, back-order management, inventory turnover, and picking productivity. Using the Rhythm software to track their movement on a weekly basis opened up a culture of transparency and collaboration on identified strategic initiatives that were of major importance to Arbill's desire to create a solid infrastructure that would sustain their growth. And this was just what they did in the *first quarter* of their transformation.

Once overall process improvement became a company goal, each department took responsibility for seeing how they could use automation, efficiencies, and general improvements to enhance the service they offer without compromising quality or the personal touch Arbill's clients have come to expect. "A clear view of our progress held each department accountable and increased transparency throughout the organization," one leader said. "Even better," he continued, "we were able to illustrate the impact that each department was having on major projects, which helped everyone feel that their contributions were making a difference."

Week by week they tracked their progress using the Rhythm software. The software gave them a dashboard that served as a repository for every single initiative they identified as being strategically relevant to the sustained success of Arbill. As a result, they could status their dashboard weekly, so that if something got stalled they could talk about solutions in real time versus getting blindsided at the end of the quarter.

The business value of transparency and creating lines of sight between what, specifically, you're doing today to get to your preferred future shouldn't be surprising. From a social perspective, transparency creates trust between coworkers and between leaders and those they lead. In a survey conducted by TINYpulse, it was found that transparency is the top factor when determining employee happiness.[13]

Arbill's commitment to using a more robust system, such as the Rhythm software, made their longer term vision transparent, and their dashboard became a repository for hosting that vision. They then linked their three-year Winning Moves to their vision, created annual initiatives that were aligned with those Winning Moves, and mapped supporting priorities across multiple departments. The thoughtful leadership paid off, as one initiative after another was executed throughout the company.

ESSENTIALS NEEDED TO SCALE FOR GROWTH

- Your culture must encourage individuals to be more proactive than reactive.
- Your company's strategic foundation should be solid, with a clearly communicated vision.
- Your organization needs to embrace a systems thinking approach that allows everyone to maximize time and energy to the fullest for the good of the entire enterprise.
- Continuous improvement of your internal systems and processes should focus on supporting an increase in profit margins (rather than just revenue) as you scale.
- Everyone in your company must understand what you're trying to do, and why, so they have context and connect to the purpose.

13 TINYpulse, *7 Vital Trends Disrupting Today's Workplace: Results and Data from 2013 TINYpulse Employee Engagement Survey*, 2013, https://www.tinypulse.com/resources/employee-engagement-survey-2013.

- Your systems should support increasing transparency across boundaries, which breeds higher-level discussions as well as a culture of trust.
- Success markers need to be identified so you can track progress on your journey from current reality to future state.
- The right talent needs to be recruited, retained, and placed in the right seats.

The Power of Cross Collaboration

As the Arbill team continued to grow their strategic thinking and execution planning strength, they realized that there was an occasional communication gap between the executive team and the next level of leaders, and that collaboration between those leaders would need to be stronger in the future. To make planning effective, they decided to involve the six divisional directors in executive-level conversations about the future of the company and the strategies needed for change. The executive team saw that engaging these division heads would help clarify the company's long-term growth plans and create alignment in thinking.

The advantage of pulling in people outside your own circle has huge rewards. Studies in social psychology tell us that people develop higher levels of collaboration and positive working relationships when they are invited to work on projects that require the various strengths, perspectives, and problem-solving approaches from a diverse team of people. In an article published by *Harvard Business Review*, Gratton and Erickson write that "the greater the proportion of experts a team had, the more likely it was to disintegrate into nonproductive conflict or stalemate."[14] Arbill recognized the value that outside perspectives could provide, and that when an inclusive culture begins cascading throughout your company, the line of sight to your vision, strategy, and more is extended. These elements become strategic operational principles that provide stability and clarity. They also saw their team collaboration on projects soar. Leaders throughout the company were learning the importance of seeing Arbill as one system versus a bunch of silos operating independently of one another. Week by week, quarter by quarter, the company began making strides toward their defined future.

Arbill's departmental directors began participating in the annual planning process and in the executive-level Weekly Adjustment Meetings. They offered solutions the company needed in order to succeed in their change initiatives. Who better to offer those solutions than the people needed to implement those future changes? The team was better informed about what was happening across the company, and why. They understood more clearly the vision and mission and why improvements in operations and cross departmental communications were important. This simple internal adjustment sped up the change process and created unbelievable cohesiveness within the leadership team.

Without higher levels of collaboration, even your greatest efforts will have limited results. A lack of effective collaboration can lead to workplace drama, and most leaders I work with grow weary of all the drama that seems to permeate the highways and byways of their companies. Growth (especially rapid growth) without a solid foundation to support it causes water-cooler conversations to go way offtrack.

14   Lynda Gratton and Tamara J. Erickson, "Eight Ways to Build Collaborative Teams," *Harvard Business Review*, November 2007, https://hbr.org/2007/11/eight-ways-to-build-collaborative-teams.

Instead of talking with a sense of engagement and positivity around results, people talk more about blame.

Most organizational drama is caused by inherent disorganization in how people are communicating with one another. As a result, confusion and duplication of effort occurs and everyone is running around doing whatever they can to keep up. Within their own silo of the organization, they're saying yes to everything because "We're growing a company!" But that only feeds the beast. Without knowledge about where a company is headed and an understanding of why something's being done or implemented a certain way, you get well-meaning people doing whatever they can with the limited knowledge they have.

"The benefits of having the directors on the planning team went even deeper into the organization," noted one Arbill executive. "They began to understand the challenges of other departments. Once they could see the adversity their coworkers were facing, they pulled together to find necessary solutions." The inclusion at the executive level helped breed a more inclusive culture at Arbill and strengthened the company. In retrospect, Julie and her team feel that increasing the size of the leadership team proved to be one of the most significant and positive adjustments they made in preparing for a future of growth.

The newly formed leadership team's open and honest exploration of their company helped them all see Arbill as an entire system, not a collection of independent silos. With a silo mentality, each separate team can inadvertently become hyperfocused on fixing its own portion of a problem, unconsciously oblivious to the effect the effort has on other teams. People working within departments at Arbill would be working on a common initiative, but each area was seeing only their piece of the work versus the entire picture. They each had their own siloed definition of what success looked like.

As an example, a hard look at the stress that growth could put on purchasing helped Arbill see that orders could be placed with suppliers, but updating the delivery information for the customer service area would need improvement, so that customer questions and inquiries could be properly answered in a swift and accurate manner. On another front, distribution could begin falling behind in receipts because they might be searching through boxes for a specific item that a customer wanted pronto. "Just these few observations told us a story about what our future would look like if we didn't continue to refine our processes as our company grew. We would have been caught in a downward spiral," one leader shared. "We had great individual teams, but they could unknowingly cause a drag on the growth that was coming our way."

To create stronger cross functional systems and efficiencies, Arbill's leadership team decided to focus on strengthening the collaboration between receiving, warehousing, and shipping. Arbill receives goods (safety products) in their warehouse and then sells those goods (either as product sales or as part of their service delivery) to their customers. And like other distributers, as Julie said, "When the majority of your revenue comes from razor-thin margins from product sales, you constantly need to keep an eye on both sales and profit." If the receiving, warehousing, and shipping side of the business isn't running as efficiently as possible, the leadership team realized the pressure on margins would be greater (and so would the ensuing confusion—which only serves to maximize drama). "Part of this deep-dive analysis into our internal processes helped us see that margins could begin to erode if growth in sales put a stress fracture in these areas of our company," Julie said.

The team decided that to accommodate hypergrowth, a massive overhaul was needed in the warehouse in order to manage costs, reduce waste and rework, and ensure a positive customer experience. As the leadership and warehousing teams began their proactive collaboration, they felt a bit overwhelmed by the depth and breadth of it all. Evolving this area would encompass numerous departments working hand in hand. One leader commented, "With multiple departments involved and a host of processes and equipment needing to be changed or updated, we struggled with where to even start."

They began by tracking their progress in simple spreadsheets, which were helpful as repositories of priorities and status. At least things were written down. They maintained those spreadsheets for a while, but as their projects became more complex and required collaboration across multiple business units, they needed a more robust system for mapping supporting priorities and tracking progress. Hitting a higher ceiling of complexity requires a more sophisticated operational approach if you want to keep accomplishing multiple goals that involve multiple departments, faster.

By further leveraging the full functionality of the Rhythm software, Arbill ditched the spreadsheets. By its very nature, the Rhythm software does what a lot of technologies simply can't do: it forces people to have meaningful conversations about things that matter. It forces a solutions-oriented approach rather than allowing a victim or an "us versus them" mentality to take hold. As leaders grow in their ability to have focused discussions about the company's overall strategic intent, Rhythm serves them by becoming the unbiased arbitrator that keeps them and other department leads focused on the KPIs and priorities that matter most *to the company*. Had they continued using spreadsheets to track these types of vast change initiatives, confusion and complexity would have multiplied as they continued to grow. Visibility and collaboration across departments would have been limited.

Arbill set priorities and success criteria for each critical aspect of their warehouse transformation and tracked progress weekly, and the teams collaborated to solve challenges as they arose. Amazingly, they didn't just meet their goals, they surpassed them dramatically. They *doubled* their pick rate, achieved 100 percent in-line order checking, reduced packaging, and improved their labeling from the customer's perspective. The project had a significant impact on their margins and their business overall.

Changing processes and improving systems that affect more than one department can feel overwhelming and stressful. It doesn't have to be that way. Breaking major annual initiatives into quarterly "sound bites" that are owned by individuals across those departments, with success criteria and timelines that help you track progress, helps fuel the company to the next level. Establishing a refined set of KPIs that helps you measure your preferences and lets you know if you're in danger of not hitting your targets tells you almost at a glance how healthy your company is. Having the discipline to track your progress week by week so that you can immediately adjust feeds energy and momentum. As noted by a member of Arbill's leadership team, "By breaking the projects down into pieces, and seeing how different people or teams were contributing to progress on those pieces, what might seem like a monumental project that would be all encompassing becomes much more manageable. And when you look at all these miniprojects, you realize you don't have to alter the responsibilities of your day job to give them the necessary attention. Now we feel like no goal is too big, that we'll be able to reach even our biggest goals."

Arbill's insightful leaders also noticed similar patterns showing up within their own newly formed team of ten, partially because of the same problems that misaligned systems would cause for each of them as the company continued to grow. They also suddenly discovered the answers to a few current challenges that had been gnawing at them over the years. For instance, they came to see that they, as leaders, each had key pieces of information that were scattered throughout different documents. There had been pockets of time when this team felt as if they were putting out fires—all because they couldn't get their hands on the package of information that was needed to readily solve an issue or a challenge. As Julie put it, "We came to see that a potential future frustration would be not having a robust way of getting to all the important pieces of information that made up the whole story. Instead, if we did nothing at all we would have a mishmash of things.

With this discovery, we could adapt in a way that would better serve us today *and* in the future."

The team was suddenly able to take a deep breath and heave a sigh of relief. They could see that moving the needle on this element of their enterprise would mean their meetings would be more meaningful and results focused. They would be able to get clearer more quickly on key aspects of their business, such as fill rates, inventory levels, and more.

Over time, Julie recognized that discussions around Arbill's future growth potential brought to light the need to upgrade systems and incorporate software to help them survive their new and promising reality. Doing this would make them efficient, which is important. However, you can be efficient all day long. The higher-level question for you to ask is: "How *effective* are we?" To be effective, they needed the insight and energy of all their leaders and all their departments, pushing forward on their most critical initiatives.

ARBILL'S MEETING RHYTHM

- **Monday morning:** Leadership team of ten has their Weekly Adjustment Meeting, which helps in several key ways:
  » Focuses their team all quarter on meaningful discussions about what's most important to the company right now.
  » Supports transparency and team thinking relative to identifying solutions and agreeing on necessary adjustments.
  » Keeps everyone aligned and moving in the same direction for the whole quarter.
  » Prevents them from getting blindsided at the end of a quarter by unexpected results.
- **Monday afternoon:** The safety advisors team has their own Weekly Adjustment Meeting after the leadership team. This allows them to get any information they might need from

> the leadership team. They're "hungry for outputs," notes Julie. "They get updates on operational changes that have happened so they can respond to a customer more in real time, if needed. If a new service is being discussed or launched, they can share the news with their accounts."
>
> - **Friday:** The operations team has their Weekly Adjustment Meeting at the end of the week. This allows them to define any "stucks" they have, and communicate those to the leadership team for a timely discussion in their Monday Weekly Adjustment Meeting.

Creating the Freedom to Focus on the Future

Julie doesn't believe in silver bullets. She does believe, however, in the power of knowing the truth, and Rhythm has led her and her team to have the tough conversations needed to grow an even stronger sense of order within Arbill and to make some crucial resource decisions.

Scaling for growth can be challenging for most any company. The stronger and more consistent your systems and processes are, the more freedom you have to work on things that will truly help you scale for growth, and the less likely it is that your infrastructure will crack as a result of that growth. How you spend your time is of paramount importance. You can spend it chasing information, in meeting after meeting, doing rework, managing unhappy customers, and watching bigger turnover than you'd like, *or* you can spend it creating operational leverage and a competitive advantage.

In line with the vision Julie and the leadership team worked to craft, they now provide a comprehensive safety offering that includes four essential verticals: safety programs, environmental health and safety solutions, safety technology, and customized safety products. As a result of this team's desire to be proactive about growth, the organization has continued to evolve into a company that can securely accept the challenge of growth with grace. They are consistently working on improving their systems and processes so that their operational foundation is strong enough to support whatever comes. Growth won't force them into inefficient operations or drama-filled frustrations. The Rhythm methodology and dashboard have facilitated the communication and messaging of what was once in Julie's own mind, while also creating company-wide transparency, focus, clarity, and alignment. So what have these things done for Arbill?

→ Total sales grew 87 percent over seven years.

→ Government sales, in products and services, grew 222.8 percent over four years.

→ Revenue from environmental health and safety programs, one of their new lines of services, grew 1,047 percent over four years.

→ Safety program revenue overall grew 53 percent over four years.

→ They reduced their past-due accounts receivable from their largest clients by 35 percent.

→ They increased customer satisfaction to an all-time high, with a more than 25 percent increase in their "Extremely Satisfied" rating.

→ Their operating expenses and general and administrative expenses as a percentage of revenue both improved substantively and are continuing to do so.

This is the type of success that most any leader would welcome. Rhythm is helping Arbill be an amazing company. It's helping them create a brand that will take them light-years beyond their vision.

It's helping them deal with the complexities of growth by having the operational and leadership processes in place to support them in their journey.

Any operational system should be designed to maximize effort and attention, thereby creating value on multiple levels for your company. Instead of being in the frenzy of rapid growth, Julie and her team have proactively taken the time to position themselves for long-term, sustainable scalability. Notes Julie, "Rhythm is allowing us to parlay our smart and talented people in a way that fosters working together to accomplish a common goal. Because of the clarity that Rhythm provides to both our operational and strategic missions, the prospects of a fourth generation leading this business going forward have never been more promising."

Indeed, Arbill is building an enduring company and an incredible legacy.

MANAGING GROWTH IS A 13-WEEK RACE

As a company scales, excellence in execution and steady improvement across the company must be a goal in order to avoid the chaos that accompanies complexity. One highly effective approach that Arbill embraces is the Rhythm Systems concept of thinking of each quarter as a 13-week race: you have 13 weeks to make progress on your annual strategic imperatives, or else you risk not successfully fulfilling a strategic priority by year-end. Therefore, Arbill uses the Rhythm dashboard to help teams together achieve more of their goals every quarter. Here's how to do this:

- Establish no more than five annual initiatives for your company (or any department or team). For each annual initiative, establish success criteria using the Red-Yellow-Green parameters. What will success look like at the end of the year?

- Next, set no more than five quarterly priorities for the company for the upcoming quarter. These should be aligned with your annual initiatives. Establish Red-Yellow-Green success criteria to clearly define what success looks like by the end of the quarter. This will create a dashboard for your 13-week race.

- Cascade the plan to departments and teams, and allow them to determine their roles in supporting the company priorities and create their own team dashboards with no more than five quarterly team priorities.

- Using your dashboards, track progress every week for each quarterly goal, and assign each priority a Red, Yellow, Green, or SuperGreen status based on completion of certain milestones and the results you are on track to achieve at the end the quarter.

- At your Weekly Adjustment Meetings, discuss priorities that are Red or Yellow with a hard focus on solving the problem or overcoming the barrier that's holding an initiative hostage. Consider anything Red as a gift revealing the need to make an adjustment in your plan now if you want success at the end of the quarter.

To download the 13-Week Dashboard Tool and learn more about the 13-week race, go to PredictableResults.com.

Big Ideas

→ To scale your company, you have to start with a long-term direction and then develop a framework for strategic thinking and execution planning that will help you steadily and predictably move in that direction. To do this, you should begin by clearly defining your vision for the future.

→ Scaling for growth requires you to methodically upgrade your management and operating systems just as you would any other system or process in your company.

→ To lead an entire company toward a preferred future, create a culture of collaboration. Doing this allows your people to begin seeing your company as one system instead of a collection of separate departmental entities, which is key to scalable operations. Collaboration also helps give them a line of sight into how the actions taken in one area impact other areas, and it increases trust, which is a core requirement for growing a healthy, drama-free company.

→ Create transparency by giving people visibility into what's most important. Scaling with focus and purpose is the best path to a bright future.

→ Use a management system that creates the right kind of accountability on projects and allows people to work together to solve problems rather than place blame. It should keep your people focused on doing what you need them to do relative to your overall strategic intent, so that you can make steady progress on your change initiatives.

→ Healthy habits and routines are the basis for a scalable management approach that will serve you well on multiple fronts and will keep you proactive versus reactive. Consider each quarter a 13-week race—and meet weekly to discuss solutions and agree on removing roadblocks where needed. Create a meaningful weekly meeting rhythm that *focuses on solutions and results*. Your ability to scale predictably depends on it.

For help developing a strategic road map for your company's growth and scalability, go to PredictableResults.com.

CHAPTER 7

DOUBLING THE CAPACITY OF YOUR EXECUTIVE TEAM

How a lean approach to leading change initiatives led to execution that was 2X faster

Barry Pruitt

Take a tour of Boston Centerless's shop floor and you will be amazed by the efficiency and meticulousness. The massive room has been exactingly designed for the most effective operation of machinery and flow of work. The equipment is placed at just the right angle, seemingly random to the untrained eye, to improve the flow of work product from machine to machine. The status of each job is prominently displayed in red, yellow, or green; there is never a question of which job should take priority, or which job comes next in line. Every employee is listed on a huge dashboard that displays their certifications. It is lean methodologies in action.

You don't have to understand lean to grasp two foundational principles of lean thinking: continuous improvement and eliminating waste. If you're in manufacturing, lean could make you best in class—or keep you there. If you aren't in manufacturing, continuous improvement as a lean practice can often offset competitive threats, eliminate waste, and create additional team-member time and greater margins.

Harvard Business School professors arrived unannounced one day to study the company and were impressed by the quality, efficiency, and total lack of chaos. I saw it myself the first time I visited—no flurry of activity, no anxiety over a looming deadline, no running to a supervisor for an answer about which job should take precedence. Instead of the chaos I've seen on so many shop floors, I saw calm, methodical progress from one task to another with acute clarity on what came next. Their efforts to eliminate waste in space, human activity, product defects, transportation, and more were evident everywhere.

For all that Boston Centerless was achieving in their high-quality production of precision metal bars for medical devices, high-performance engines, and the like, the leadership team wasn't satisfied. Those amazing efforts I saw on the shop floor to ensure that each job got completed with minimal waste and to incredibly exacting standards weren't happening at the executive level. Rather than a clear idea of what project should take priority, they had a list of eight to ten objectives each year. Rather than a clear standard of success for each objective, they had a general sense that they should be making progress and getting more done. Rather than a strong quarter-by-quarter execution plan, with a way to easily track progress, CEO Steve Tamasi felt the burden of "enforcing" accountability and maintaining an antiquated spreadsheet. When he was too busy, each leader's day job took precedence and some things simply didn't move. "As hard as our team worked and planned," Steve told me, "we'd get to the end of the year and say, 'We were going to do all these great things. We only did two out of ten.'"

The waste they had routed again and again through continuous improvement in manufacturing was ever present at the executive level and slowing their progress on strategic initiatives. As the CEO, Steve was wasting time and energy tracking down the status of important projects and making sure things got done, and even then, they didn't always. Without precise execution plans, the team was wasting opportunities to have the right discussions week after week, quarter after quarter—discussions that could help solve problems, identify opportunities for improvement, and move the company forward faster. Imagine any one project being discussed weekly by five senior team members for only fifteen minutes. That would equal one hour and fifteen minutes of leadership time for a minimum of 65 hours annually. In the previous year, Boston Centerless had more than five key initiatives incomplete at year-end, equaling hours of labor and weeks of work, with disproportionate results for a large effort. With lack of clarity on priorities, the company was wasting resources and executive capacity pursuing too many objectives, which inevitably meant that some were abandoned after money, time, and other critical resources, including executive brainpower, had been spent.

To break the pattern, reduce waste, and improve the ability to accomplish goals and hit targets, the team needed to scale their executive-level execution processes to keep up with the quality of manufacturing their company was known for. When we first began working with Boston Centerless in 2012, Steve had already led the family-owned company to quadruple its sales over the past decade by focusing on systems and standards that would drive growth and efficiencies. He had rebuilt the executive team to bring on expertise in running a larger company. But he didn't have any tools or processes in place to effectively and efficiently drive execution of their long-term strategy. He needed a way to increase focus on the right few strategic initiatives, drive better discipline in the team, easily track status and progress, and delegate confidently so that more could be accomplished faster.

To break the pattern, reduce waste, and improve the ability to accomplish goals and hit targets, the team needed to scale their executive-level execution processes to keep up with the quality of manufacturing their company was known for.

Executing 2X Faster to Stay Competitive

Boston Centerless's executive team knew they needed to make fast progress in a few critical areas, based on how the industry was changing and what they were learning as they expanded and improved their offerings. New equipment and competitors tightened a market that wasn't growing as quickly as past years. The executive-team processes, however, were insufficiently aligned with the new market paradigm and need for rapid transformation. Steve was committed to changing that.

The first area for improvement was their sales and marketing systems. If you have ever tried to drive sales transformation, you'll know it is never as easy as you think it will be. In a good company, the sales process is tied to almost every other department in one way or another, and transforming it usually affects the entire company. Steve and his team were faced with myriad changes.

Consider the complexity of what the team at Boston Centerless had to accomplish. First, they needed to implement a medical device sales and marketing plan to better focus on that growing market in a way that aligned with current research. And they needed to adopt and implement a new customer relationship management (CRM) system that would align sales efforts with manufacturing capacity and project management. Those two initiatives alone would be enough for most teams, but Steve and his team knew they couldn't stop there. They also had to support marketing and sales of their new product and service offerings by testing and deploying stronger branding efforts. At the same time, they needed to respond to customers' desire for a more user-friendly website. And to top it all off, it was time for them to create a sales playbook with a redesigned sales process, improve their quoting processes to support higher sales targets, and develop and deploy a new training program for their sales team.

This was not something that could be accomplished in a quarter or two. It was not something that could be quarterbacked by one person. It would require the coordinated effort and innovation of multiple teams week by week, quarter by quarter, year by year. And while it was happening, the critical day-to-day work of the sales team had to continue, and the company had to respond to ever-shifting market conditions. The antiquated spreadsheet approach they had been using to track projects and Steve's role in enforcing accountability could not support the complex initiatives they needed to complete—and complete as fast as possible. But Steve and his team had already found a better approach, and this massive initiative would be the perfect test of their newly implemented Rhythm methodologies and software.

First, they needed a thoughtful plan that was focused and aligned on the most important priorities, thereby eliminating wasted efforts. Then they needed appropriate accountability for individual efforts and a way to quickly identify progress toward agreed-upon results. Every quarter I worked with Steve to develop and document a solid execution plan, which included clear priorities for individuals that would push the initiatives forward, success criteria for those priorities, and appropriate completion dates. The underlying message for the team was that they needed to get on top of this. It seemed at first that they found it painful to discuss accountability and commit to clear measures up-front, yet those discussions led to solid adjustments throughout the quarter. (You can read more about the Plan Rhythm in Chapter 5.) Confusion about what needed to be done by whom and when almost disappeared.

The clarity of the plan improved the quality of team discussions and the efficiency of their decision-making. First, clear success criteria made Weekly Adjustment Meetings easier, and second, the focus of discussions for anything Yellow or Red was moved from status discussion to solution discussion. The conversation became "What can we do to get this moving toward success?" rather than "We're currently falling short of the goal." Solution discussions helped the team coordinate efforts and resources across disciplines and reduce duplicate work. And they established success criteria for key performance indicators (KPIs) that would help them gauge their progress week by week and keep them focused on critical numbers while executing their Winning Moves.

For example, one KPI was the sales opportunity pipeline. This was important, yet risky if all opportunities came from one customer. The countermeasure was a KPI measuring diversity and balance of opportunities among clients and prospects. With both items on the KPI dashboard, the executives could balance team-member efforts.

Using Rhythm software, they began tracking their progress on individual, team, and company priorities and KPIs. Transparency on status, reviewed at Weekly Adjustment Meetings, improved their flexibility by helping them quickly spot defective components of their plan and make appropriate adjustments. And progress was no longer dependent on Steve's bandwidth for driving accountability. "Once the plan is in place," he told me, "people are self-directed. The system does the managing, and I don't feel like I have to ride herd. If I get busy and I don't have time to follow up, it will still get done." And with a stronger focus on solving problems rather than enforcing accountability, discussions became safer and more productive while morale improved.

In the middle of the transformation, they faced a setback that every leadership team faces. An executive left—the sales executive. Worse, after months of hunting for an appropriate new team member, they were disappointed to discover that their (almost) new hire had lied on his resume and they had to restart the process. They couldn't just halt progress, so the head of operations took on sales leadership and the sales process improvement initiative. Because of the history of the projects, the clarity of status, and the defined steps in Rhythm, he was able to step in and keep the transformation moving forward. When you lean out your executive leadership processes, it's easier to hand off responsibilities as the team changes and grows along with the company.

Quarter by quarter, piece by piece, the team at Boston Centerless dramatically improved their sales processes and their management and leadership processes. For Steve, the newfound speed of execution, with a streamlined approach to managing objectives, has changed his perspective on what's possible. "If we had not had a tool or process like this to structure those activities, I can assure you, we would not have been as successful in implementing that project. It just would have dragged on."

5 WAYS THE EXECUTIVE TEAM CAN APPLY LEAN

1. Lead with Purpose: Determine elements of your core strategy, such as BHAG, core purpose, and core values; publish them, and then stop wasting resources on people or opportunities that do not align.
2. Continually Improve Your Leadership Processes: Apply continuous and never-ending improvement weekly. Create a team to identify underproductive processes and empower that team to initiate improvements. When the team solves a challenge or improves a process, they should move on to another.
3. Build a Culture of Problem-Solving: Foster effective problem-solving skills by creating designated think time and using Weekly Adjustment Meetings to keep plans on track. Use probing questions like how, why, and what to get to the root

of an issue. Make sure your teams are focused on solving problems, not assigning blame.

4. Provide Role Clarity: Formalize job scorecards to give each team member clarity around what is expected of them and a framework for driving out waste and redundancy in their daily work. (For help, download the Job Scorecard Tool from PredictableResults.com.)

5. Make Performance Dashboards Visible: Create dashboards of the most important things for teams and individuals to focus on. Make sure these dashboards are public and updated with the current status of each KPI or priority. These dashboards will help keep discussions focused on results and solutions necessary to improve performance.

More, Better, Faster

No leadership team can work on just one strategic initiative or Winning Move at a time. It takes movement in multiple areas of the business to drive consistent, predictable growth. While the Boston Centerless team was working on the sales transformation, they were also upgrading communications systems throughout the company. They were also expanding geographically and developing ideas for their next Winning Moves. Today, they are in the midst of transforming their supply chain approach in order to improve their competitiveness in key markets. Each complicated process change requires commitment, consistency, and discipline, and Rhythm reinforces those ideals. With Rhythm, leaders can feel confident that the right work is being accomplished by the right people on the right timeline—a timeline that is always shorter than it would be without it. "In every instance," Steve has proclaimed, "*our objectives are happening two times faster.*"

Their improved Plan Rhythm, with a focus on execution, refined KPIs, and communication quarterly and weekly throughout the company based on success criteria and dashboards, has helped reduce waste and delay, improve quality of execution, and bring energy and focus to the strategic priorities throughout the company. Methods they have used to bring clarity, steadiness, and predictability to the shop floor for 20 years are now being used at the executive level to coordinate the work on long-term strategy. Steve put it in the most fitting words he knew: "Rhythm has leaned out the process of executing company priorities."

The Big Ideas

→ As you scale your company, you must also scale the capacity of your executive team to keep pace with the demands of the business. While adding executives may be necessary, make sure your current team is working as efficiently as possible first.

→ If you want to reduce wasted time and opportunity and improve the functioning of your executive team, you need a process for identifying priorities, clarifying targets, and tracking progress that can expand as you grow.

→ Signs that your executive management processes are out-of-date include executives feeling torn between their day jobs and strategic priorities, a CEO who feels it's necessary to enforce accountability, and strategic initiatives that aren't getting done or that are moving forward far too slowly.

For tools and insights to help you work on your executive team processes, go to PredictableResults.com.

CHAPTER 8

MAKING ACQUISITIONS WORK

How clarity, accountability, and the right metrics helped a company double its size and dramatically expand its reach

Tiffany Chepul

It wasn't the first time Bill Koeblitz and the rest of the leadership team at MobilityWorks had considered an acquisition. Over the past decade, they had acquired eleven small companies, each with a handful of locations; they felt they had the hang of it. With this opportunity, though, they would significantly change the size, geographic spread, and potentially the future of the company. With one acquisition, they could add 21 stores to their existing 35 and expand their presence all along the East Coast.

Bill and his team weren't oblivious to the statistics on mergers and acquisitions predicting that it probably wouldn't be a success. They understood that 50 to 90 percent of the time (depending on the size of your company or the study you're reading), an acquisition fails to deliver the growth in revenue or the improvements in profitability the leaders expect. The outlook is so gloomy, experts in the field advise people to explore every option for achieving their strategic goals before they settle on the M&A route.

And they had done that. Bill, a car fanatic for his entire life and an entrepreneur in the health care industry, had founded the company in 1997 with one shop and a vision for providing independence for people with special vehicle needs across the country. In just 18 years, MobilityWorks had become the largest retailer of wheelchair-accessible vans through smart, steady, organic growth—as well as acquisitions—often moving into markets with no dealer or owner base and building a successful store from scratch. They had developed partnerships with some of the best manufacturers and suppliers in the industry. And they had launched a commercial division that had become Ford's biggest mobility upfitter.

But now they were discussing acquiring a publicly traded company, HASCO Medical, Inc. (the parent company of Ride-Away and Mobility Freedom dealerships), which came with higher costs and greater financial risk than any strategic move they had made in the past. This was, by far, their largest acquisition. Bad deals are certainly a killer of good acquisition outcomes, but even when the financials make good sense, leaders have to deal with a host of other challenges:

→ Is the acquisition a good Winning Move based on the company's long-term strategy, or is it a distraction?

→ Are the cultures compatible, and is there a system in place for reinforcing the culture?

→ Do the leaders have the capacity to manage the necessary work and the chaos of integrating two companies well, or are they overburdened with solving existing challenges?

→ Are they prepared to communicate, communicate, and communicate some more in a way that keeps the entire team, existing and new, aligned on the vision and focused on the right results?

→ Do they know how to go about integrating the companies, do they have a clear process and discipline in applying it, and do they have a system for knowing whether it's working or not?

Bill had taken a serious look at the health of the company prior to moving forward. He felt they had the first criteria well in hand: sufficient capital to fuel the acquisition and sustain them through the integration. "If the existing business needs X amount of capital to weather a storm, plan on having 3X available for the existing business, the acquired business, and the unknown issues," Bill told me when we were discussing the plan. He was also confident in his leadership team: "Highly effective leadership must be placed at the acquired business to handle unexpected twists and turns. And those leaders must be totally free from responsibilities at the existing business in order to be effective."

HASCO was a primary competitor in some of their markets—a strong, respected company with its own culture, systems, and embedded relationships between corporate leaders and the general managers responsible for the success of each store. There was a lot of potential for confusion, doubt, and resistance. But Bill and his team knew that it was a good culture fit, because they had been operating in some of the same markets for years. If they could get the integration right, make it happen quickly, and create as seamless a transition as possible for the people in the HASCO stores, they could achieve something great.

Companies that have a strong execution cadence and a system for sharing their strategy, aligning their teams, and communicating expectations with priorities and key performance indicators (KPIs) can avoid acquisition disaster. MobilityWorks had strong rhythms and tools in place; pairing them with a disciplined focus on making the integration happen quickly and successfully has helped them achieve aggressive goals. But what specifically did it take to make it happen?

Companies that have a strong execution cadence and a system for sharing their strategy, aligning their teams, and communicating expectations with priorities and KPIs can avoid acquisition disaster.

Build a Foundation for a Much Bigger House

One day in 1996, Bill Koeblitz walked into a struggling mechanic's shop and discovered the perfect business—growing market, clear customer base, alignment with his personal passions. It was like Frankenstein's lab, and it fascinated Bill, who had grown up racing Fiats and rebuilding car engines before he shifted gears and became a CPA. He watched as mechanics worked to cut a van almost in half and then rebuild it piece by piece while adding custom components to make it wheelchair accessible. In this garage that had fallen on hard times, he discovered the potential to improve the lives of hundreds, if not thousands, of people. He had a vision for expansion from the very beginning.

To start, though, he had to overcome the flaws he spotted amid the promise. The investment by customers was massive: they had to wait months to get the vehicle, there were no standards or laws to ensure the passengers would be safe in a crash, and the conversions were a bit ad hoc. If he wanted to have a profoundly positive impact, he would have to improve operations and deliver a consistent level of quality, safety, and experience.

It took five years to complete that initial, all-important step. At the first MobilityWorks store in Akron, Ohio, they worked on perfecting inventory, systems, safety, quality, value, and the customer experience. Finally, in 2003, they felt ready to open a second location in Detroit that focused on sales and service. Later that year, Bill made his first major acquisition and added four locations, in Toledo, Pittsburgh, Albany, and Canton. In 2006, he hired Eric Mansfield to oversee operations at all the locations and push for consistency. By 2010, MobilityWorks had 14 stores—and they had hit a wall of scalability. Each store seemed to have different strengths and weaknesses.

Each manager had his own personal selling style. Certain locations or regions were constantly struggling. If Eric wasn't frantically trying to solve the day's big problem, he was lying awake at night wondering what the next issue would be.

It's a basic truth of scalability: there's no way to profitably add locations, team members, products, or services—organically or through acquisition—if managing the current ones is killing you. As Juan Alcacer, professor of business administration at Harvard Business School, has said, "When you open a new operation, it requires not only money but also the time and energy of managers to make sure it's going the right way, and that means you can't focus as much on the base business."[15] Eric finally went to Bill and said, "We can't keep doing it like this. I don't know what we need, but we need to do things differently." What they needed was to reinforce their foundation with a core strategy, rhythms, and tools that would improve visibility and predictability, and they needed to sharpen their focus as a company.

They began working with the team at Rhythm Systems to implement methodologies and tools for strategic thinking and execution planning—annually and quarterly. They clarified their core strategy, refined their goals, and used the Rhythm software to begin tracking their progress on priorities and key performance indicators (KPIs). Each week, they measured and updated their status and became comfortable with the discussions and accountability that comes with defined parameters of success and a push toward quarterly priorities. "The 13-week race of execution changed things dramatically for us," Bill told me recently. "We were able to get the right things done consistently. It took away a lot of the anxiety." Anxiety that they didn't want to increase as they added new stores.

....

15 Dina Gerdeman, "Location, Location, Location: The Strategy of Place," *Harvard Business School Working Knowledge*, January 9, 2012, http://hbswk. hbs.edu/item/location-location-location-the-strategy-of-place.

In 2011, MobilityWorks hit all-time highs financially, but Eric was exhausted. He was now overseeing 20 locations and they were beginning to realize a flaw in their hiring. Bill didn't really think of MobilityWorks as a vehicle sales business. He thought of it as a path to changing people's lives for the better—and still does. Eric's first experience with MobilityWorks paints a similar picture. He was looking for a more inspiring career, and at a trade show, he watched a dad and his daughter find and purchase their first van that would accommodate her wheelchair. The joy on the daughter's face and the relief and happiness on the dad's were overwhelming. "I wept like a baby that night," he told me.

Not surprisingly, they hired people with the same values and drive to help others. They had a lot of nice, good-hearted general managers (GMs)—many of whom had a deep personal connection with the business because they had a family member or friend who used a wheelchair. But they weren't car salespeople, and that fact was creating problems. During the executive team's planning for 2012, they made the choice to invest $1 million in people and build a stronger sales organization, adjust their structure to take some of the weight off Eric's shoulders, and offer better support and development to the GMs. Their decision to add regional managers with deep experience in car sales led them to hire David Wolfe, a lifelong car guy—his dad had owned a Dodge dealership and David had spent 25 years in the industry. David's success in growing the sales strength of the company—their solution rate has improved by more than 60 percent over the last few years—has proven that the investment was a smart one.

Consistently, through this work, they emphasized their culture and purpose. Take that solution rate. Most companies like theirs might call it a close rate, but at MobilityWorks they believe it's their job to solve the problems that keep people from the vehicles they need. Their brand promise—"Our caring professionals will provide custom mobility products unique to your and your family's needs and that fit your family's budget. We will support you 24 hours a day, 7 days a week"—isn't simply words on a wall in the break room. They set aggressive goals for customer satisfaction and track the KPIs closely, store by store. Their execution rhythm, including weekly meetings of regional managers with their GMs, emphasize solving problems and supporting one another by sharing knowledge and points of success.

David, who is now a divisional manager, told me recently, "We have built a foundation on which we can build a really big house." A good thing, since they set an ambitious long-term strategy of dramatic national expansion. Year by year, they worked on that foundation because they understood that without it, new additions could collapse. And if they got it right, they could use it to educate, align, and inspire new employees and teams that came onboard. More important, though, is that the foundation made them less anxious, their results more predictable, and the performance of each store more visible. The visibility and predictability expanded their confidence, resources, and leadership bandwidth. In fact, their first regional managers were responsible for four or five stores each. Today, with their improved execution rhythms and management operating system, they can handle ten. They would need access to that energy and those resources to make a major acquisition possible. Of course, having the foundation isn't enough. In an acquisition, you need to give people a way to connect to it, to see that the cultures truly are compatible, and to align their work with the right results.

IS YOUR FOUNDATION STRONG ENOUGH TO SUPPORT AN ACQUISITION?

- First, do you have enough capital on hand to support the existing business, the acquired business, and the unknowns?

- Is your leadership team currently stretched too thin, or do the executives have the bandwidth to provide highly effective leadership at both the existing business and the newly acquired business simultaneously?

- Do you have clear core values and a core purpose that will help you successfully maintain your winning culture? Are they in action, day to day, or are they words on a plaque?

- Do you have well-defined KPIs—both leading indicators and results indicators—that will clarify expectations for all existing and new employees and give you visibility into the success of the acquired business in real time? (Download the KPI Creator Tool and the Leading Indicator Creator Tool from PredictableResults.com.)

- If you are acquiring a business that does what you do, are you confident that you are doing it well, especially if you expect the new teams to adopt your approach or processes? Have you fine-tuned your own business to organically grow your market share?

- Do you have a management operating system in place that drives good execution, supports predictable growth, and is easily scalable?

Figure Out the Right KPIs to Keep a Pulse on Existing and New Revenue

Eric called me one day in the fall of 2013 after their quarterly planning session. "We've figured it out," he told me, his voice full of energy. "We've figured out our magic formula."

We had been working on refining their KPIs quarter after quarter. When we began working together, MobilityWorks had been tracking

17 measures of company success, and many weren't valuable, predictive enough, or driving the right behaviors at the store level. If the primary focus for each store is gross profit per employee, for instance, what will a GM do if his numbers are off target and he can't boost revenue? He'll probably look for ways to cut costs, such as reducing the head count or level of service, which can then make morale drop, turnover increase, customer satisfaction decrease, and gross profit take a bigger hit.

Progress was a process, but we eventually narrowed their KPIs down to a shorter, more powerful list tied to critical goals and financial targets. Next, they needed KPIs that would help them develop a predictable sales engine at the store level—and after a year of working on them, they'd had a breakthrough. During the quarterly planning session, the team had listened to a few customer calls that had come through a new call center. Those calls and their improved focus on sales helped them understand the sales *process*, which happened in three simple steps: (1) a person made an appointment, (2) she showed up for that appointment, (3) she discovered a vehicle that fit her needs and budget and bought it. Their magic formula of sales KPIs to improve predictability became simple:

→ Number of appointments, a leading indicator
→ Appointment show rate, a leading indicator
→ Solution rate, a results indicator

Step by step, improving these three measures leads to higher gross profit at the store level and company level, a key financial indicator, but they also maintain the team's focus on helping customers through the process. (If you aren't sure whether your KPIs are helping you drive growth, download our *KPIs to Drive Your Business* guide from PredictableResults.com.) Just as important as identifying the right numbers and building accountability for them was giving regional managers and GMs ownership of those numbers. Even something as simple as logging into a system, entering a number, and commenting on the status of that number rather than having your boss do it for you can be emotional and motivating.

At their Weekly Adjustment Meetings, GMs discuss their status on their critical numbers and their priorities and get help from their peers when they're stuck. Giving them the power to own their KPIs and to see how their peers are doing across all locations helped improve results, because employees who own their numbers improve their numbers. Visibility into and accountability for success at the store level helped establish clear expectations, drive the right behaviors, reinforce the culture, and create a sense of community across stores.

David said to me recently, "What Rhythm does for us as a company is to let everybody know where they stand, where they should stand, and what the goal is. There's never a doubt about what they should be working on." Imagine the power of this approach and clarity for those 21 new GMs coming onboard, who might be full of doubt, worried about working for a new regional manager, uncertain about what's expected of them and whether they'll know if their performance is on target. Being part of an acquisition is never a comfortable thing, and that discomfort doesn't fade until you know exactly where you stand in the new company or with your new leaders. The best thing we could do for the new GMs was to get them working with the Rhythm software and train them on the Rhythm cadence as fast as possible.

I'll be honest and say that when I got the call asking me to set up trainings for the new team members, my stomach did a little flip-flop. I wasn't sure what kind of resistance I might face. But Eric and David seemed completely unencumbered by the worry that most people in their situation would be feeling. They knew we were ready, and they were right. In my calls with the new GMs, I heard again and again that most of them had never operated with this level of focus on clear performance indicators, much less with a proven "magic formula."

From day one, they knew what was expected of them and they knew they would be supported; there is tremendous power and peace in that. Within three months of the acquisition, they were statusing each KPI, developing the habits, and participating in Weekly Adjustment Meetings. It took some time for them to become comfortable discussing their Yellows and Reds—most had never participated in Weekly Adjustment Meetings designed to help them solve challenges rather than blame them for less than optimal results—but over time they embraced the positive, solution-oriented culture.

The clarity and the cadence quickly helped build the best kind of alignment and focus with new team members, which kept the company from wasting resources or losing revenue while integrating the HASCO stores. It helped that every GM is accountable for the same results, which puts new and old on the same level and builds a sense of unity and cohesion. And the work that MobilityWorks did to develop their core values, core purpose, and other aspects of their culture, as well as their core strategy, comes through in their cadence and the tools they use—it's all in the Rhythm software for the teams to see. Even when cultures are compatible, you need to give new team members a way to see that they do fit, to understand how they are doing, and to connect with the new culture in an inspiring and uplifting way.

For the executives at MobilityWorks, the visibility they had developed into the performance of each store offered valuable insight as they integrated the "New 21," as they were called. They could quickly spot which GMs needed more support, training, or coaching in specific areas by clicking through and seeing the results on KPIs and the progress on priorities for each store. David, who was responsible for assessing the strengths of the new stores and training the GMs, could watch their progress week by week, spot the need for additional training or support, and work with the appropriate regional manager and GM to discuss a strategy to get the store on track. And he could do that work proactively, thereby avoiding being blindsided at the end of a quarter.

In the first quarter, we saw a lot of Red weeks on the dashboards for the new stores, especially when it came to that critical number, the solution rate. But in the second quarter, those Reds regularly turned to Yellows and Greens, and even SuperGreens. After just six months of serious integration effort, by the start of the third quarter, most of the new stores were producing results similar to the original stores. Was there still room for improvement? Of course. The company still isn't hitting its goal for its overall Net Promoter Score (NPS, a composite KPI that includes the score from every store). But as you might guess based on what you've learned from their culture, their goal is incredibly aggressive: an NPS of 80 percent. Most companies would kill for a score 20 points below that. Even Apple's iPhone division hovers around 70 percent. But the results overall have been inspiring—by the end of 2016, their overall NPS was 79.3 percent, pretty close to that ambitious goal. For the leaders at MobilityWorks, it was further proof that their culture, approach to the sales process, and reliance on a strong execution cadence had the power to produce the right results.

BEST PRACTICES FOR INTEGRATING NEW PEOPLE INTO YOUR WEEKLY EXECUTION RHYTHM

- Explain in clear terms how each priority and KPI helps predict or track success, is aligned with company growth initiatives, and is measured each week.
- Structure Weekly Adjustment Meetings so they are a mix of existing and new employees.
- Make your Weekly Adjustment Meeting a safe environment. The KPI is Red, not the person—especially new people or

teams who may feel anxious and may need some coaching to get to Green.

- Model good habits. All existing employees should be communicating the status of priorities and KPIs, and commenting on hurdles they're facing weekly to help new employees see what drives successful adjustments.
- Spend extra time celebrating the SuperGreens and looking for Bright Spots—good ideas that can scale. Give tenured employees more time to talk about how they achieved success or got past Red. Their insights can help new employees move faster.
- Get new employees the help they need when a KPI or priority is Red or Yellow. Develop a plan ahead of time for who will be responsible for coaching or sharing company wisdom, outside of regular meetings. When new employees feel supported, they'll be more transparent and engaged and hit a successful stride faster.

Make Integration a Priority and Give It A Lot of Energy

When you are about to execute what is possibly the most aggressive Winning Move in your company's history, you cannot leave anything to chance. You cannot hope that the most important things get done. You plan, plan, plan. You develop a clear path to execution that includes every necessary team member, every critical step, and then you reinforce the plan with as much energy as you can possibly devote to it. And that is exactly what MobilityWorks did.

It began during their annual planning session for 2016. They established a theme for the year—the primary focus of the company for the next 12 months—that included "successful integration of the New 21." One of the five key initiatives they identified for the year was "develop and implement integration of the New 21." In the first quarter of 2016—which had a theme of "sustaining momentum through change" to help maintain focus on the company's goals while teams devoted energy to the integration—the number one priority for the company was "integration of the New 21." The Energy Map in Rhythm, which is a dashboard that shows the number of related team-level priorities for a company priority, revealed a host of focused activity by various teams devoted to making it happen—far more than any other priority for the quarter. Supporting priorities like "develop and implement GM mentoring program for New 21 GMs," and "facility rebranding" also had their own support in the form of individual actions.

David and his team held much of the responsibility for the integration. "My plan was to get to each store quickly, create a very positive first impression, and express that the new team members were going to be an integral part of our company going forward," he explained to me. "They had to know that we had a training plan and know that I was responsible for it." David was also responsible for establishing the GM mentoring program. "I needed to provide them all with a support network of existing staff so they knew who to go to to get answers to their questions."

He updated his progress in Rhythm, including comments on key dates and deliverables, decisions that the team had made, and dependencies on other priorities. He explained what had been accomplished, his plan for rollout, decisions about having the new GMs spend time in the stores of their mentors, and deadlines for each phase of the program. All team members understood where the program was at all times. If anybody needed information about the program to understand how it tied into work they were doing with the new GMs, it was all easily accessible.

The work continued into the second quarter, of course, when "integration of New 21 stores" was still a top three company priority, with solid energy backing it. In the second quarter, the focus of team priorities was on implementing MobilityWorks's rental service into the new stores, refocusing the training programs based on what the leaders had learned about each region's unique needs, and improving the solution rate in those stores that were still struggling to meet MobilityWorks's high standards, including an action item to daily monitor the solution rate for those stores and have follow-up calls with the GMs to discuss solutions. Now, that's discipline and devotion to executing for success.

There was no confusion about what needed to happen, how much energy it would require from individuals and teams, or when it needed to be completed. Adjustments were discussed weekly to keep the plan on track or to change the plan if the team learned of new needs in the New 21 stores. Nobody got distracted by some new idea or opportunity, abandoning the necessary work and possibly ruining the success of the integration. By the end of the first quarter, the new stores were aligned with MobilityWorks's systems, processes, and approaches to sales and service. And by the middle of the second quarter, MobilityWorks's overall solution rate, including results from all the stores, was very close to what it had been before the acquisition. By the end of the second quarter, their gross profit from consumer sales had met or exceeded their projections for each quarter since the acquisition.

The acquisition was so successful, and the team's handling of the integration built so much confidence in the leadership team, they decided to pursue three more acquisitions in 2016—yes, three more!—which added five stores to their roster in April, four in August, and three more in September. They had a well-defined process for integration, a team devoted to making each store a success, and a system and rhythm that made it easy to execute the plan and support each new store and each new leader.

• • •

Bill Koeblitz and his team are incredibly proud of how MobilityWorks is steadily fulfilling its core purpose of "Making the world accessible!"

"We are able to take care of over half of the people in the US," he told me. "We stretch from coast to coast." And they're doing it while maintaining a strong focus on trying to deliver a buying experience that creates real value for the customer. All because they've built the foundation, the rhythms, and the discipline to acquire, execute well, and scale without missing a beat. They are one of the rare few who have beat the odds.

What's next for MobilityWorks? A renewed focus on their foundation. They are a dramatically larger company than they were a year ago, and they want to revisit their core strategy to make sure it's still compelling, consistent, and strong enough to keep adding on to their house.

The Big Ideas

→ If you're considering an acquisition as a Winning Move to push your company forward, check your foundation first. Is it strong enough for the addition? Every acquisition requires substantial time and effort from leaders. If your leaders are overburdened with challenges and foundation building, they won't be able to devote the time and resources to the acquisition that will make it a success.

→ Visibility and clarity are critical requirements of a successful acquisition. You need clearly defined KPIs and priorities that will help the acquired teams understand exactly what is expected of them and how their work fits into the overall plan for the company. And you need the ability to track their progress, week after week, to understand how the integration is going and where you need to devote more time and resources. Otherwise, you may not realize for months that things aren't going as planned.

→ The right set of KPIs that drive revenue in a predictable way is key to sustaining the existing business and driving the right behaviors of new employees. Identify a "magic formula" that fits your business model.

→ Integration of an acquisition is a complex project. Coordinated effort from a variety of teams and individuals, applied with discipline, is the only way to make it happen. You need to create a detailed execution plan that hits on every critical piece of the process, sets clear criteria for deliverables, and allows people to track and communicate their progress so that everybody is informed and aligned.

→ The entire organization can support the integration process by training and modeling strong quarterly and weekly execution rhythm habits. They help clarify expectations and provide a consistent process for accountability when things can feel chaotic.

For tools and insights to help you build the visibility, clarity, and efficiency you need to support successful acquisitions, go to PredictableResults.com.

CHAPTER 9

MANAGING GLOBAL TEAMS AND ENGAGING REMOTE EMPLOYEES

How one company brought leading-edge technology to the global market with a virtual office that kept high-performing teams aligned across borders

Ted Skinner

In 2012, MarketLinc was sailing directly into a perfect storm of business chaos. Don Simpson, founder and CEO, and his five executive team members sat in a hotel room in Boston, trying to settle some of the biggest decisions in the company's history.

The technology they relied on to provide their product—providing superior inside technical sales support to their customers—kept getting bought up by other companies and then orphaned, leaving MarketLinc scrambling to find a replacement. They were a regional organization based in Canada, and the unemployment rate in their area was plummeting because of the energy industry boom—great news until you are trying to hire the talent you need to meet your customers' needs. And they could foresee a major shift in their industry looming on the near horizon.

At some point over the last few years, you have possibly interacted with a MarketLinc employee and not even known it. If you have pulled up a website, browsed for a while, and were then prompted to chat or talk with a person who is there to help, you're seeing the kind of human-to-human digital commerce support MarketLinc offers to companies like Norton, Kaspersky Lab, and Citrix. In 2012, they could see the trend toward, and possibilities in, online human sales support, but if they wanted to create a growth strategy based on it and capture the interest of global customers, they would need to build their own platform, broaden their services, and change their value proposition. All those big Winning Moves would require them to reach far beyond their current geographic boundaries to build a stronger team via a virtual office. Their success and growth to that point had been based on the strength of their tactical work, almost all of it happening at their headquarters, but they understood their future success depended on the leaps they would make in developing their strategic planning, alignment on priorities, and day-to-day execution with a dispersed team.

Getting complex initiatives accomplished as a team is difficult. When you're not in the same building, city, or country, it can be much, much more difficult. More and more, though, companies are building their teams across borders and time zones to take advantage of talent pools around the globe or to build a brand presence in local markets. For these companies, every challenge comes with an additional layer of complexity—complexity that can increase errors, off-target or duplicate work, and lack of connection with the big picture of what the company is trying to accomplish. This can slow them down and make it difficult to break through growth ceilings.

As companies go beyond geographic boundaries to recruit great talent, expand into new markets, or adjust how they make or deliver products and services to achieve their dreams and goals, they need new systems to support communication, alignment, and engagement within their virtual work environment. Managing dispersed teams and engaging remote employees is not easy with traditional communication tools and processes. It's difficult to feel connected to the team by email and the occasional phone call alone. It's difficult to trust that the right work is getting done on the right timeline. It often feels like the big picture goals get lost and the culture is fragmented. Leaders can feel pressured to micromanage from a distance. Employees and teams can suffer as well. How do you replace the happy collisions in the office that build personal connections when using electronic communication? How do you battle the disconnectedness that comes with operating in different time zones? It's easy for remote teams and employees to become silos, lack opportunities to offer their expertise, not understand how their work fits in or how they can contribute to the work of others, and lose sight of priorities.

MarketLinc understood the risks of the virtual office they were developing, and knew that if they were going to continue to be successful, they would have to nullify them. They couldn't find all the talent that they needed to push beyond the next growth ceiling and had to expand their geographic search to find the best in the world. As Mark Mortensen, a professor of organizational behavior at INSEAD and an expert in global teams, describes in a *Harvard Business Review* article, physical separation can create two primary problems: (1) social distance, which affects team dynamics and can create an "us versus them" mentality, and (2) lower levels of mutual knowledge or context. "A shared sense of context, a shared understanding of not only what you do but how you do it and why," he writes, "is a key driver of your ability to coordinate and collaborate. Teams with a shared understanding are more efficient. They don't waste time ensuring everyone is on the same page and they have fewer issues with miscommunication."[16] When you're innovating, mutual knowledge or context is essential.

The most successful dispersed teams we've seen use their business execution system to support individual and team focus on the right priorities; effective, timely, and targeted communication; and a sense of connection across teams and between individuals throughout the organization. If you're struggling to create these essentials in your organization, you need to assess the systems you've put in place at all levels. Does your executive team plan effectively and then transparently communicate priorities with everybody in the organization to build the right foundation? Is it easy for departments to communicate and collaborate on cross functional initiatives? Are your teams getting regular—and I mean weekly—feedback on their progress to help them focus? Are people connected with the vision and strategy?

MarketLinc worked to tackle these challenges right from the start of the shift in their business model by using the Rhythm methodologies and systems to build the right cadence and environment. They understood their future would depend upon effective, efficient, coordinated work on big initiatives, which is what they had always prided themselves on. To make their teams as successful as they needed them to be, they worked hard to make everybody feel a part of the spectacular business they were building. "I feel like more than an employee here, and I have never seen any of these people in person, let alone been in the same country," wrote one reviewer on Glassdoor. That sense comes from relevant information shared broadly, and visibility that breeds collaboration, support, and steady progress. With that kind of energy, they have pulled off some of the most complex initiatives and powerful innovation, positioning themselves among the very best

16   Mark Mortensen, "A First-Time Manager's Guide to Leading Virtual Teams," *Harvard Business Review*, September 25, 2015, https://hbr. org/2015/09/a-first-time-managers-guide-to-leading-virtual-teams.

The most successful
dispersed teams we've seen
use their business execution
system to support individual
and team focus on the right
priorities; effective, timely,
and targeted communication;
and a sense of connection
across teams and between
individuals throughout the
organization.

in the world at predicting and reporting incremental revenue from digital engagement efforts with customers.

Achieve Your Most Important Initiatives by Getting Everybody Working on the Right Things

Don Simpson, CEO, and his small executive team gathered in a hotel room, faced an incredibly tough decision: Do we move ahead with our existing business, or do we substantively transform the business? They wondered if it would be worth the angst and effort. One of the company's core values may have tipped the decision scales. Innovation has been a central tenet of the company since it was founded, and sticking with what they were currently doing and hoping the market sustained their business certainly didn't seem innovative. So they made the tough, exciting, and frightening choice: they would build their own software platform, one with a wide range of service options that set them up for the best possible future.

They started simply in that hotel room: they mapped their strategic vision on a piece of paper. One element of that future vision was to have their daily execution bound to their strategic planning by 2015. That would become a challenge as their team grew and expanded geographically. But to innovate the way they needed to, they couldn't rely on their local talent pool.

MarketLinc needed to remove a large constraint that was keeping it from being the company it could be: the geographic constraint to hire the best talent in the world, the global A players who would help drive their vision and brand. Without those A players, MarketLinc might have been overwhelmed by the waves of change in their industry or failed to achieve the possibilities they saw in 2012.

Throughout 2013 and into early 2014, they were deep into

building the software engine to support their vision while they grad-ually built their management team. They were transitioning from a sales and marketing service company to a highly regarded, dispersed global technology company with an innovative product and distinctive promise: customers can use MarketLinc's tools to determine where human interaction will be most powerful and pay MarketLinc *based only on the increased revenue they generate.*

By the spring of 2014, complexity was increasing exponentially as they ran pilot programs with key customers, added more and more A-player managers in more and more locations, developed operations in India, Brazil, and elsewhere, and faced their next major hurdle—moving their platform and all operations into the cloud while con-tinuing to innovate. They had been satisfied so far with the success of their remote teams and employees, but the complexity was starting to wear on them, and they wanted to get ahead of the even greater complexity they knew was coming. They needed a much more robust virtual office for their ever-growing team, one that would help them achieve that alignment between strategy and execution, and they found it in Rhythm.

The team had begun using the Rhythm methodology on paper in 2012. They met annually and quarterly to develop strategic goals, initiatives, and execution plans. Those methods had helped them build their execution muscle, and they had accomplished more in two or three years than many companies could have. But with the expansion of the team, they needed something more robust than a spreadsheet to maintain alignment across teams and to improve visibility for the executive team.

One of the biggest challenges of leading dispersed teams and remote employees is feeling confident that people are working on the right things. As a manager in a different city or continent, it can be easy to feel disconnected from the larger goals of the company, or to not understand what you should be doing this week or this month to support those goals, or where to focus the efforts of your team. It's easy for teams to feel like islands, and when that happens, they begin to make their own choices about what's important. Being able to confidently answer the question, "What's the most important thing for me to work on today?" can be difficult even when you aren't spread around the globe. When employees don't have a good answer to that question, you end up with a lot of effort wasted on the wrong things and negative surprises at the end of a quarter. Your job as a leader is to coach your people and teams to success. How are you going to do that proactively if you aren't sure they understand what they should be working on? What you need is a systematized strategy connector, because micromanaging from another continent is definitely not a great way to spend your time.

"I think in any business, it's helpful to be able to align everything that's being done," Don told me recently. "In a virtual business, even more so. Everybody interprets things a little differently. Having to document and define your goals and priorities and record them all in one place forces you to clarify your thinking and your communication, which is really important. To be able to say, 'Here's our annual plan. And here's what our annual initiatives are.' And then have them flow through, on a quarterly basis, to answer the question, 'What do we need to do to make sure we're accomplishing the plan?' And then meet every week to ask, 'Okay, where are we at?' And to all be aligned. Because each one of these things we've worked on is a heavy, *heavy* lift. To be able to keep everything aligned every quarter and every week—who wouldn't want that?"

That focus and alignment, supported by the Rhythm methodologies and tools, was possibly most crucial in their transformation and migration of their software and all operations to a cloud-based platform. It is the most complex multiyear initiative they've tackled in the history of the company, especially because it was paired with advances in their software that dramatically improved their ability to report incremental revenue generation to their clients—a critical piece of their competitive value proposition. I think of the initiative as comparable to trying to work on the engine of a car that's driving 55 miles an hour down the highway. They had to maintain excellent service for their clients while working on the underbelly of the technology that allowed them to provide service to those clients. And when they kicked off the project in late 2013, they had already spent more than a year reinventing the company once, releasing a new technology, adjusting their services and marketing, and staking a claim in their new industry with their ability to identify the best opportunities to optimize digital engagement and increase revenue.

The MarketLinc team met to develop their plan annually and quarterly, and then met weekly to discuss progress and any needed adjustments across multiple departments to match the progress of the software development team—based on the thousands of moving parts across their organization and in the marketplace. The communal software for tracking annual initiatives, quarterly priorities, and actions, as well as connected comments, kept people who were working on positioning and marketing plans in Brazil, adjusting sales forecasts in Vancouver, dealing with financial certifications in San Francisco, or supporting IT infrastructure improvements in India firmly aligned. Their agile approach to business execution allowed them to make decisions based on the latest information from all corners of the company, which significantly increased their chances of success. More important, though, everybody in the company understood exactly where their focus should be, week by week.

Of course, it didn't always go as planned—what serious endeavor ever has? Don used terms like "frustrating," "onerous," and "knocked off course" to describe parts of the odyssey. It took longer than they had planned, their current customers were anxious for the new platform and getting restless, and they couldn't onboard new clients until the migration was complete. Knowing what a powerhouse of planning the MarketLinc team is, I can't imagine what this project would have done to a less aligned and driven company. But MarketLinc has had a crystal-clear vision since 2012 to build the world's best human-to-human digital engagement platform, and they weren't going to let up until they had. Their steady Think, Plan, Do Rhythms that created time to discuss progress and hurdles weekly and quarterly, even if the people meeting weren't in the same room or on the same continent, made adjustments possible, because everybody was aligned and had extreme clarity on what was most important.

Although it wasn't easy, in the end, they accomplished exactly what they set out to do. They are ISO and SOC II certified (the latter proves that the company's system is keeping clients' sensitive data secure) and are audited by PricewaterhouseCooper regularly. Gartner, an industry leader, released a report on best practices for measuring your incremental revenue based on optimization activities, and the only intellectual property touted in the paper other than Gartner's was MarketLinc's.[17] They essentially described MarketLinc's approach as the way it should be done. Most important, MarketLinc's Intelligent Visitor Engagement Solution is delivering significant incremental revenue for its clients. With a consistent track record of strong performance, the big household-name companies they were building all this to attract (à la *Field of Dreams*) are sitting up and taking notice.

Over the next few years, now that the foundation and value have been developed, the MarketLinc team expects their growth to explode. They're continuing to push toward that growth with incredible quarterly gains in their operations, their relationships with customers, continued improvements in their platform, and development of their sales and marketing teams. All these efforts require a tight focus from

---

17 Martin Kihn, "Use A/B and Multivariate Testing to Improve Marketing Programs," *Gartner*, September 1, 2016, https://www.gartner.com/doc/3431917/use-ab-multivariate-testing-improve.

dispersed teams, and their steady stream of successes prove that focus is happening.

Keeping a dispersed team on track to achieve goals together requires leadership discipline, but a centralized system for communicating in real time eases the burden. I read an article recently on the topic that offered tips for managers, including defining team goals and creating a path to those goals, making sure feedback is consistent, and setting up an online team page or portal where members can share ideas on projects.[18] These tips are helpful, but achieving more initiatives, and more complex initiatives, requires a much higher level of focus and alignment, supported with robust systems, across departments. Everybody needs to be on the same page, with the most up-to-date intelligence, and clear on their role in contributing to the success of the initiative.

"Everybody's pitching in, in a different way, to achieve that overall objective," explained Don. "Of course, the communication cycle of constantly reviewing our progress and asking, 'How are we tracking?' makes all the difference. And as we learn from feedback in the market, every day, we share that to tweak our messaging, our sales process, our product. That constant communication with our executives and managers helps us make sure that we get this right, or as right as we possibly can." Even with their successes and the strength of their systems, they are always working toward improvements. One of their annual goals for 2017 is to build a "cross functional playbook to run the business like a Swiss watch."

Similar to how we feel connected in social tools, the right management operating system can provide an open collaborative space for all employees to engage and understand how their goals align with the

---

18   "Managing a Geographically Dispersed Team: Achieving Your Goals Together, While Apart," *MindTools*, https://www.mindtools.com/pages/article/newTMM_40.htm.

company strategy. The result is less time spent managing, the potential to lower your overhead costs, and better outcomes due to improved focus, alignment, and accountability. I would say MarketLinc is one of the most successfully dispersed companies I know; their unified work on incredibly complex projects has shown it. While their management system has brought Don peace of mind, efficiency in management, and visibility into their progress as a company, it has brought every team member the clarity and surety they need to keep successfully completing initiatives week by week.

Stay Speedy with Real-Time Communication from All Stakeholders

One of the common complaints—or fears—of managing dispersed teams and remote employees is the time cost. Even in today's hyper-connected world, leaders worry about the extra time it might take to communicate with people who aren't in the same office, the excessive attention to email it might require, and the repetition of goals and priorities in phone call after phone call. The result could be wasted management time, slower progress as a team, and delayed response to changes in the market, in the industry, with partners, or within the company.

At MarketLinc, the establishment of the marketing and sales teams is a perfect example. In 2016, MarketLinc, at that point more than 25 years old, didn't have a marketing team, but knew they would need one. As their transition to the cloud was nearing completion, they knew it was time to begin seriously ramping up their business development, marketing, and sales efforts. So in February of 2016, they hired Paul LaRochelle, based in Vancouver, away from SAP where he was a Global Vice President and 20-year veteran, to become their senior vice president of business development.

Over 18 months, they built a team to support their market transformation across two continents and three countries. "Just to get six or seven people singing off the same song sheet of value proposition, who we are, the vision of where we're going as a company, the market we want to serve—that can be hard to do, right?" said Don. Absolutely! And yet it hasn't seemed to slow them down. Rhythm Systems helped them onboard new hires at least 30 percent faster than they ever could have in the past. They were quickly able to see where the company was, where it was going, and the core values it cherished.

MarketLinc began working on a brand refresh to align with their new value proposition. Early in 2016, they launched it. In the second quarter of 2016, they began work on a complete website redesign based on the brand refresh, including all new market-vetted copy, a new messaging framework, new videos, and new case studies. In October, they launched that, too. By late summer, they had new market segments defined, new personas developed, new targets identified. They had expanded their relationships with industry analysts. They had developed a new client acquisition process. And they had completed these incredibly complex maneuvers in amazing time (I know companies that have taken two years just to launch a new website) through their high levels of alignment and visibility.

Utilizing Rhythm gave MarketLinc the ability to view the new branding rollout as the large cross departmental project that it was—just as they had been able to with the new software platform rollout. Sure, most of the pieces were being developed by the marketing and business development teams, but the sales, service delivery, and website teams were affected by the project as well. Again, just as with the shift to the cloud, every person in the organization felt the impact. Without a system for reporting and coordinating, they might have faced a complete lack of visibility, and other teams would be vulnerable to being blindsided at any turn.

The individual and team priorities and actions in Rhythm for every aspect of these intertwined projects were robust. In the fall of 2016, one company-level quarterly priority focused the efforts of marketing, sales, and business development, calling the three an "engine." Within that priority was a list of eight team priorities assigned to team members. Within each of those team priorities were individual priorities and critical actions with milestones or deadlines assigned to those team members.

Speed of execution requires the right information at the right time to make the best decisions possible for the right projects. The information has to be relevant to your work and to team goals, and aligned with what's most important to the company—you shouldn't have to wade through a flood to find the streams you really need. Information has to be easily and immediately accessible (no waiting for the other hemisphere to wake up), efficiently organized by project, initiative, or priority (no hunting through email to find a critical comment), and clear and shared transparently (no silos of information within departments). Without this approach to information and communication, everything slows down, error rates rise, and profitability takes a hit. This is much more true when employees can't supplement the information they're getting with a quick visit to somebody's office or an overheard hallway conversation.

We hear a lot about collaboration in the business media these days, but the foundation of all collaboration is transparent sharing of information. Too many dispersed teams rely on information-sharing approaches that are barely functional for teams sitting within feet of one another. Or they think adding a chat-based tool will help improve knowledge sharing. What they miss is the importance of having a single system that supports all relevant and critical information about every project, in an asynchronous format, and that maintains a full history of every initiative. Historical detail helps people understand the source of decisions or adjustments, so that they can make better decisions going forward and avoid making the same mistakes that were made in the past. And effective, focused, targeted communication about what's happening this week or this quarter helps people adjust quickly to changing circumstances to maintain progress toward their goals.

At MarketLinc, every person on every interdependent team working on the rebranding initiatives could see the progress of every other person on every other team—through the related key performance indicators (KPIs), the status of their individual and team priorities, the comments on those priorities, and more—creating absolute clarity on each of the related deliverables, goals, priorities, or hurdles. Leaders reviewed the status of all priorities on Monday mornings before having their Weekly Adjustment Meetings with their teams to discuss how to solve any challenges, eliminating any and all silos. That unparalleled visibility generated incredible speed. "Everybody's a sprinter," said Don, "but to win the race, you've got to hand the baton off to the next person when they're going at full speed, and you can't toss the baton."

That was just as true in the major innovations the company was working toward: keeping everyone in the loop and focused on the most important work of the week or quarter. Those running the pilot programs shared insights into client needs that helped the developers improve their work and helped marketing refine their initiatives. Sales stayed updated on the progress of software development. Marketing was able to get better insight into the vision of the company and customer needs to better refine their new branding initiative. Visibility into the pilot programs that were building the bridge to the future while keeping an eye on their current clients helped other departments shape their work to support success. It was a massive multiyear project that relied on the success of interdependent priorities. And even though it took years, and longer than they expected, it would have taken much, much longer if they hadn't been so deliberate.

One of Don's favorite stories of speed of execution concerns an internal platform switch. Their goal had been to fully integrate marketing, business development, and sales into a single system. One of the hurdles, they realized, was a platform they were using for a couple of those teams to manage the sales funnel and more. "We came to the conclusion that to make everything clear, tight, and completely integrated, we would be better served working with a different platform." They already had priorities pushing toward these goals, and so the decision to move—a midquarter adjustment—was made within two weeks. And the move was completed three weeks later. "We were able to communicate the decision to our product management and IT people and help them understand it in very, very short order, because we have that clarity and collaboration on what we're trying to accomplish for the year and what our quarterly goals are and the hurdles we might face. Instead of it spinning our wheels for months, we made it happen in about three weeks."

Don shared with me the essence of one of his favorite quotes about the benefit of using a system like Rhythm: "It brings things into the sunlight, and sunlight is the best disinfectant."

Visibility from the top down throughout the organization and from the bottom up to the executive level is important, but so is visibility across departments. It creates cohesion, improves efficiencies and effectiveness of teams, and helps build an understanding of and respect for work being done by others. And all those things reduce waste and increase an organization's speed of execution.

EXECUTING WITH SPEED: THE ESSENTIALS

- Executing with speed is not about having the perfect plan; it's about focused effort and making the right critical adjustments along the way.
- Making the right adjustments requires absolute clarity on top priorities and KPIs to create focus and shine a light on problems.
- Weekly Do Rhythms, such as Weekly Adjustment Meetings, keep everybody aligned, accountable, and engaged in the process.
- Focus your meetings on problem-solving and doing work, not just on updating one another on the status of your current list of projects.
- Consistently updating and making visible the status of priorities and KPIs keeps individuals and teams accountable and focused on making steady progress.

To watch the webinar "How to Get Your Team to Execute Faster than the Competition" and to download the 13-Week Dashboard Tool for communicating progress on your priorities, go to PredictableResults.com.

Keep Your Talent Engaged with More Frequent Feedback

Retaining top talent is a challenge every company faces. For remote employees, it can be even more difficult. How do we engage people in the culture? How do we help them connect with the big picture purpose of their work, which we know is a major factor in motivation?

How do we empower them to raise their hands in a visible way when they need help or have a great idea?

Everybody wants to feel a part of something bigger at work, wants to understand how they're contributing and why their work matters, wants to feel in the loop and connected to the leaders and their peers. But when you're a remote employee, it can be easy to feel like a silo of one or three or ten, like you're on a somewhat lonely island. Rhythm methods and tools help build teams, relationships, and cultures across boundaries by emphasizing the connection between teams, to the strategy and vision, and to what's happening in the organization in close to real time. When you build this approach into your company, don't be surprised when your employees hold you to it.

When the cloud-based transformation was getting close to complete, the executive team made a choice. The project had taken longer than they expected, which affected the company's ability to onboard new clients for longer than they expected, which impacted their overall results for longer than they expected. In short, the company was off target. Typically, at the end of each quarter, after planning for the next quarter has been cascaded throughout the teams and completed, Don does a recap for everybody in the company: here's what happened last quarter, here's what we're doing this quarter, here's how we're tracking on our annual initiatives, here are our successes so far. He uses Rhythm dashboards and other tools to tell the story of the company and show the aligned goals and collaborative work being accomplished. Well, amid the push to get the transformation complete, onboard a couple of new executives, and deal with some off-target results, Don and the team didn't go through that round of broad communication.

The response was quick and negative. "People were frustrated," Don told me. "We did an employee survey and got feedback saying that our communication was slipping. If you're using the tools and communicating consistently, folks are happy and feel good about what's going on, even when the news isn't everything they might want to hear."

As one study found, feeling like you're a part of a cohesive team is critical to engagement—92 percent of engaged employees scored positively on questions about working together as a team.[19] Engagement at MarketLinc is high, especially for a company with an almost totally virtual office, because Don gets it. "The consistency of the Rhythm process and having everything aligned is very reassuring for people. They know where they stand. They know what the company's about. They know what the plans are." Because everything is right there in Rhythm, including the core values, the Big Hairy Audacious Goal, the long-term initiatives, and the quarterly priorities.

And when those plans and priorities are fulfilled, everybody can celebrate because everybody understands what they mean to the company and what hurdles had to be overcome and adjustments had to be made to see them through. As a senior employee said in one conversation, "We said we were going to do this, we did it, and you can see what we've done. I think it just makes those wins more meaningful. It's like, 'We said we were going to run an Olympic race and get the gold medal, we trained for it, we ran it, and we came home with the gold.'" Day-to-day accomplishment across the organization, communicated regularly, is inspiring and engaging. And even day-to-day challenges, communicated regularly, are engaging.

The cadence of the Weekly Adjustment Meeting helps people stay informed and participate in important discussions, but it also gives them an opportunity to raise their hands and say, "I need help," or "I have a better idea." In these discussions, the feedback loop is shortened to a week, while in some companies it could be a month

19 TNS, "8 Tips to Engage Your Employees," *TNS Employee Insights*, 2014, https://www.qualtrics.com/wp-content/uploads/2014/06/TNS_2703-14_ManagerTipsBook_EMAIL.pdf.

before you discuss your progress on a critical piece of an initiative with your leader or with your counterparts in other departments. Employees can also help where their skills or experience are needed, and have an outlet or environment to see where that might be, which can be a particular challenge in globally distributed companies. People and teams are accountable for their results, but also for everything they can bring to helping the company succeed. And that feels really good to engaged employees.

With the growth of the company in the last few years—their management team has grown from 31 people in 2012 to 71 people in mid-2017—getting new employees engaged with the vision, purpose, and strategic direction of the company has been critical. New employees who don't entirely understand their role, what's happened before they arrived, or the big picture of the company can't contribute effectively. At MarketLinc, the most critical information about the big picture of the company is all in one place, on one page. Faster and more effective onboarding keeps execution running at top speed and engages new employees faster, improving your return on payroll faster.

"If you are not individually motivated and independent, working remotely may feel challenging at first. Give it some time, you'll find a connection with people within the communication tools after a bit," wrote one person on Glassdoor. This connection comes from a focus on engaging people through systems and methods designed to help people engage, be accountable, and participate, no matter where they are.

ENGAGING DISPERSED TEAMS AND REMOTE EMPLOYEES

- Use video whenever possible. Video conferencing is extremely cost effective and studies have shown that it boosts engagement with remote employees.

- Start all meetings off with a round of good news to keep the energy up and remote team members connected and engaged in the successes of the company overall.
- Use virtual collaboration tools, such as Rhythm, to add accountability to actions assigned during the meeting and to maintain momentum between meetings.
- Make sure your systems and communication tools are designed to help remote team members understand the company's vision, their team's purpose, and their roles within it.
- Meet in person whenever possible. For executive teams, make sure that the team gets together for at least quarterly and annual planning.
- Don't skip Weekly Adjustment Meetings, even when multiple team members are traveling or on vacation. Establishing this discipline will provide a sense of connection and continuity that helps employees feel part of the bigger picture and helps them engage with new ideas and challenges.

• • •

Today, MarketLinc is solving a major challenge for its customers by identifying visitors who need more than a digital experience and forecasting how much incremental revenue can be generated by delivering it at a world-class level. In a recent audit for one customer, the difference between what the audit showed in incremental revenue generated by engaging certain segments of customers with a MarketLinc sales specialist and what their automated system said would be generated by that effort was 0.11 percent, which is remarkable. The industry standard for a margin of error in reporting incremental data is 10 to 15 percent. Their platform is successfully targeting the right customers and predicting the value of engaging them. MarketLinc's relationships with their customers are growing stronger every day as both their technology and inside sales team proves their value in segmenting customers, automating what can be automated, and increasing revenue. And quarter by quarter, they're improving their platform based on new research and new data.

MarketLinc's pride in their team and their success in creating a virtual office that really works shines through in their verbiage, such as statements like "We believe in the way work should be," "We are a meritocracy that values input at every level," and "We lead the path with remote employment." These and other key phrases highlight their belief in the power of this future of work. Given what they've accomplished over the past few years, they should believe; they have a highly innovative, value-creating technology, an amazing leadership and management team that has more than doubled in size, an industry-busting ability to measure incremental revenue from online engagement efforts, and a deeply developed functional organization based on their profound willingness to look anywhere for the right talent and experience.

"Our future is bright," declares one headline. With this aligned, engaged, and innovative team, that's a guarantee.

The Big Ideas

→ Great execution with a globally dispersed team starts with good systems and methods for communicating the vision and long-term strategy of the company, planning quarterly and annually, and tracking progress on initiatives *weekly*.

→ Keeping remote employees working on the right things requires clarity on a plan for the quarter and individual and team priorities aligned with that plan. The more complex the initiatives—with interdependent, cross departmental work required—the more important having this type of clarity and specificity is.

→ Being proactive in how you lead dispersed teams and remote employees, and how you communicate their roles, their purpose, and their most critical priorities, will help you eliminate waste, avoid errors, and improve your profitability.

→ Too many dispersed teams rely on information-sharing approaches that are barely functional for teams sitting within feet of one another. Working with teams spread across countries and continents can slow you down if you don't find a way to maximize the efficiency of your communication. All leaders and managers need access to timely, targeted, relevant information—information about what's happening now and what's happened in the past that they can use and share with their teams.

→ Everybody wants to feel a part of something bigger at work, understand how they're contributing and why their work matters, and feel in the loop and connected to the leaders and their peers. If you want to hire and retain A players who are going to operate at a distance, you need to get them engaged with your vision, values, and strategy early and often.

Centralizing all that information and tying it to your current strategy and their priorities can get them up to speed much faster and help them connect with purpose.

→ Remote employees need opportunities to engage with the broader challenges of the team and offer their expertise and ideas. They also need an opportunity to raise their hands to say they need help.

For tools and insights to help you engage dispersed teams and remote employees to achieve more of your important initiatives, go to PredictableResults.com.

CHAPTER 10

DESIGNING A CULTURE TO GROW WITHOUT DRAMA

*How sustaining the right culture helped increase
both revenue growth and employee happiness*

Melissa Enriquez

"In the beginning, we thought, *We're going to be nice, we're going to treat people well, and that will be our secret sauce.*"

This was Deborah Michael's inspiration for founding North Shore Pediatric Therapy in Glenview, Illinois, in 1999, according to David Michael, her husband and company cofounder. Like her colleagues, she did not like the private practice where she worked as an occupational therapist. She felt stifled, unhappy, and believed there was a better way. Deborah knew the only way to bring her vision to life was to open her own business—"a place where I'm going to treat the employees well, people are going to grow and be happy, and the clients are going to be happy" is how David described her vision. Her solution was to create a practice that was uncommon in the health care industry—a multidisciplinary pediatric therapy clinic—with a staff that loved to come to work to help kids and change lives every single day. She thought this would be the perfect environment to attract the best kind of pediatric therapists. And she was right . . . at first.

Over the next two years, Deborah established the supportive and safe environment she envisioned and hired her first two occupational therapists; they had more clients than they knew what to do with and hardly any space. Five years later, the company was booming, with double the square footage at the original location, two new larger locations in Chicago and surrounding towns, and new occupational, speech, and physical therapy services. But drama had started to surface.

As North Shore continued to grow organically, they needed more infrastructure to support their therapists. They had no formal management structure, and it was taking a toll. They were a growing business with new challenges and responsibilities that took therapists away from seeing their clients, impacting productivity. There were new clinics and staff to align with the original clinic. It was a lot to handle and they needed some direction. "The company was going to implode," David explained. "There was a lot of tension. People were working independently and doing their jobs well, but with no direction, no leadership, no one to report to. The company just grew without any infrastructure. It had to be led by somebody, so either I needed to leave my medical practice, or we were going to have to find someone from outside to come in and lead it. And we didn't know how to do that."

This was a critical moment for North Shore, so David decided to quit his job as a physician to support the growing business and become CEO. It was time to focus on building a more robust management and operational infrastructure if they wanted to continue to grow—and they did.

But by 2006, there was more negativity than they could bear. The pressure on therapists to help support the growth of the organization had increased. People were swimming in different directions, creating waves for everyone. It was clear that North Shore needed to make some dramatic changes to maintain the growth they desired.

They had hit a classic "culture chasm," according to David Niu of TINYpulse and Mark Roberge of HubSpot. They shared their research in a *Harvard Business Review* article in 2017, in which they show that most companies experience a chasm between happy employees and revenue growth a handful of years after they start up. As revenue growth accelerates, employee happiness falls.[20] And the faster the growth, the lower the happiness scores. With everything we know about how happy, engaged employees contribute to the success of an organization—revenue, profit, innovation, and more—this is a real problem for growing companies. It was easy for Niu and Roberge to track the decline in start-ups, but midmarket companies face the same problem, especially if they haven't been paying enough attention to culture.

"We started in November of 1999, and from that early point I don't recall having a single strategic thought about culture," David reminisced. "You can't just be a nice person and treat people well, and then have an amazing culture and everything is fine and dandy. Culture is made up of more than that. You need to have systems, you need to have management, you need to have structure." But you also need to have the right people, who are aligned with your values and purpose. That year, North Shore's strategic move was to get rid of the negativity.

"I took advice from a mentor," David shared, "and we terminated a significant number of staff—even ones who were highly loved by their clients and were performing well in terms of their productivity. But their attitude stunk. We needed to get rid of the negativity because we wouldn't be able to develop the culture with those people creating waves for everyone." The company took a substantial revenue hit, but the team knew it was too risky for North Shore to keep these people

20 David Niu and Mark Roberge, "How Morale Changes as a Startup Grows," *Harvard Business Review*, March 24, 2017, https://hbr.org/2017/03/how-morale-changes-as-a-startup-grows.

onboard if they didn't have a commitment to the success of the company. The people leaving told them that they were going to fail, but they knew it had to be done if they were going to build the kind of company they believed could keep growing.

It helps when your bold moves are proven through results, and at North Shore they were. In the year after they took the revenue hit by removing the negative therapists, their growth curve increased. "You could see it," David said. "A big dip down and then a much steeper growth curve from that point forward." And bold moves like this create clarity for those who remain, by sending a definite message that positive attitude and contribution to group success are more important than the money you bring in the door.

Leaders of midmarket companies share a running refrain: "We don't know what happened to our culture." It isn't easy to sustain a culture in which employee happiness and a drive for growth are given equal importance. And the rise in negativity, disengagement, and lack of purpose that often grows along with the company can seem impossible to solve. That problem then becomes a serious threat to growth. One employee engagement survey from Bain & Company of 200,000 employees found that "engagement levels are lowest in sales and service functions, where most interactions with customers occur."[21]

Leaders sometimes think that creating core values is enough to give them an engaged team and consistent growth. But what they don't always realize is that culture is a mix of people and process, and as both of those things change, the culture can evolve in ways that they didn't plan or didn't want. As David has put it, and as North Shore

---

21   Jon Kaufman, Rob Markey, Sarah Dey Burton, and Domenico Azzarello, *Who's Responsible for Employee Engagement?* (Bain & Company, December 11, 2013), http://www.bain.com/publications/articles/whos-responsible-for-employee-engagement.aspx.

Design processes and
establish systems that
put your core values, your
purpose, and your desired
outcomes into practice
weekly, even daily. If you
can do that, you will build
accountability, engagement,
and ownership.

now states on their website, there is a big difference between culture by default and culture by design.

First, you need the right team. Then you need to design processes and establish systems that put your core values, your purpose, and your desired outcomes into practice weekly, even daily. If you can do that, you will build accountability, engagement, and ownership—and your happy team will drive your execution for growth in ways you never thought possible.

Build Your Foundation and Align Your Team

How many times have you heard leaders say they struggle to find time to "work on the business" because they're so busy "working in the business"? This is a discipline that I learned early on in my career, realizing that it is a vital part of growing a scalable business. Recognizing the need and actually making it happen, though, can be two very different things.

At North Shore, David had the same realization as he stepped into his CEO role. For him, the first step was recognition—he recognized that they had not been strategic about their culture. In fact, he will tell you outright that their culture problems were partly caused by their lack of leadership and management infrastructure. It didn't feel good to have to let go of so many people, even though they knew it was the right thing to do, and they wanted to avoid having to ever do it again. You have to spend time "working on the business" to influence the culture that you want. It's that simple, but not easy.

"You do need to take time to think about and envision what you want your company to look like," David shared. "If you walked in in the morning, what would you see? How would people be behaving, talking to each other? What would the atmosphere and the feeling

be? And then you have to think about how you're going to get there."
With this mentality, David and the team established a Think Rhythm
to work on developing North Shore's core values and purpose—
their core ideology. These are critical elements of any company's core
foundation.

Purpose:

To experience the joy of bringing happiness into the lives of children and their families.

Core Values:

→ Nonstop growth

→ Stay invaluable

→ Positive attitude and high performance

→ Think solutions and get results

A common cause of culture problems is a disconnect or communication gap between the leaders' vision and expectations and those of
everybody else. If you haven't defined or communicated your purpose,
vision, values, and long-term goals, then you aren't sharing the core
elements for the culture you want. As you develop them, you have to
consider how they will support your growth and the happiness of your
people—or you might not get either of those things.

Communicating them isn't enough, though. We've all heard
that. You also need processes and systems that help you bring them
to life. In 2009, David made the decision to bring Rhythm Systems
into the business to help their team get focused on and aligned with
their growth goals. They began by establishing quarterly priorities and
key performance indicators (KPIs) that helped clarify their vision for
growth, guided by their core strategy. These pieces were visible to all
leaders in the Rhythm software. They also clarified their focus on therapist productivity, the driver of their financial engine, by tracking it as
a KPI for each location. These may not seem like important steps in
culture building, but engaged employees are informed employees who
are aligned with the direction of the company and understand how

they contribute to it. In the article where they describe the "culture chasm" in start-ups, Niu and Roberge also explain where leaders can start proactively and strategically building their culture: "We found that one significant driver of employee happiness is the employee's rating of *management transparency*, showing a stronger correlation with company culture than factors like benefits or work-life balance."[22]

For David, Rhythm offered something more than communication, clarity, and transparency. Early on, he saw a connection between North Shore's core values and the value of the Rhythm approach to the team. "Rhythm is all about projecting and planning for your growth," he explained, "so we're putting in front of us a visual of our *nonstop growth* quarter to quarter with the goals we establish and track." Each leader has priorities that they helped create and Red-Yellow-Green success criteria, which helps them see how they are *staying invaluable* week by week, and how they are growing. At their weekly and quarterly meetings, they approach discussions with a *positive attitude* and energy and reflect on their numbers to stay focused on *high performance* and *getting results*.

Many of my clients use Think, Plan, Do Rhythms and Rhythm software to help solve different business-growth challenges, especially alignment of their teams. The platform, they've said, helps promote healthy, honest, low-drama conversations about where you are as an individual, a team, and a company—and where you need to be. A few years ago, during a period of leadership change, the team stopped using Rhythm for several quarters, not realizing the effect it might have. Maria Hammer, North Shore's current CEO, shared, "It really changed the structure of our company, not being able to track our

----

22   David Niu and Mark Roberge, "How Morale Changes as a Startup Grows," *Harvard Business Review*, March 24, 2017, https://hbr.org/2017/03/how-morale-changes-as-a-startup-grows.

KPIs, our company goals. Everything fell apart. We will never do that again."

Regardless of your values, transparency and alignment can be a crucial part of any good culture building, especially as you grow into a more complex organization. If you're struggling with a culture chasm, evaluate the systems you have in place. Are they promoting the behaviors and values you envision?

7 QUESTIONS TO HELP YOU DISCOVER YOUR CORE VALUES

1. Which few people in your company do you think best represent what is good and right about your culture?
2. What stories come to mind of these individuals behaving in a way you admire?
3. What underlying values do you think might be driving their behavior in these stories? (Start a list.)
4. Who are a few people who didn't work out or fit well in your company?
5. What values do you think may have been present or missing in these individuals? (Add to your list.)
6. What patterns do you see when you study your list? (Narrow your list to five to seven core values.)
7. After sharing this list and getting feedback from others in the company, determine if this list passes the test.
   - Would you fire someone for not living these values?
   - Would you take a financial hit in order to maintain them?
   - Are they alive and visible in your culture?
   - Do they describe the personality of your culture?
   - Can you imagine using these words in daily discussions?

If you can answer yes to all these questions, you've nailed it. If not, keep refining your list and your language until you can. To help you work through this process, download the Core Values Discovery Tool from PredictableResults.com.

The Power of Focusing on Culture in Your Strategy

Having core values and other elements of your culture defined is one thing, but actually putting strategic focus and execution planning in place to ensure the entire organization embraces them is a whole other ball game.

At the beginning of 2012, this was top of mind for David. Their growth was continuing at a rapid pace. In 2010 and 2011 alone, they added social work and neuropsychology specialties, developed and were accredited for providing continuing education for therapists, went to paperless charts, and began accepting insurance, and the number of new clients *per month* more than tripled. They had plans to increase their number of therapists dramatically over the year. The pace of growth was so fast, David knew the culture—and their ability to continue to grow with purpose—was at risk if they weren't proactive and strategic about it.

They started by determining their focus for the year. Their number one business issue to address was maximizing productivity while maintaining an excited culture, so they established a primary annual initiative: "Focus on our core values and building a strong team of dedicated staff." They wanted to establish the core values more concretely throughout the organization and encourage behaviors that embodied them. They then built an execution-ready plan that included individual and team priorities that focused on maximizing productivity and bringing their core values to life.

For the first three quarters of the year, their top two priorities were to improve both the employee and the client experience. Experience is a lot about culture, and improving it for employees would increase both their happiness and their productivity, and improving it for clients would increase revenue. For each of these company priorities, they established individual priorities to bring focus and energy to the necessary work. The most important individual priority in the first quarter designed to support the improved employee experience was "encouraging core values behaviors." Throughout the quarter, they developed and rolled out a program for peer-to-peer recognition of behaviors aligned with the core values. In the next quarters, they improved their onboarding of new therapists to help build alignment with the culture early.

Creating priorities helped the team execute strategic plans to proactively sustain their culture. They continued to build the right systems internally to get the behaviors and culture they desired. Over the years, they supported therapists' professional growth by launching a deep cross discipline training program and continuing education courses, which they enhanced and improved year by year. In the training program, they spent time on their core values, purpose, and key elements of their business that supported their culture. They developed manuals and mentorship programs. To this day, the team continues to be creative about designing processes that embody their core values and purpose to sustain the culture they desire. For instance, they capture Magic Moments, or moments when a staff member anticipates a family's need before they recognize it themselves and then surprises and delights them with it. Internally, staff members recognize one another for these moments, and contests help promote this behavior throughout the company.

If your culture needs your attention (and it almost always does), make your focus known and put a stake in the ground. Stay committed. During your planning, make sure the priorities you establish are aligned to support improving elements of your culture. If you don't have priorities for culture, then how will your employees stay focused or know what is important? You have to be purposeful when designing your execution plan. Then, set up your dashboards with clear success criteria and see the work in action every week. This will drive accountability and focus and get results—especially on activities that can be overshadowed by the growth fire of the day.

As major forces behind the culture and growth of their company, David and Deborah decided it was time to fulfill a lifelong dream of theirs to move their family to Israel. They wouldn't have been able to do that if they didn't have confidence in their team and their systems for executing these critical priorities. They moved in 2012—how awesome is that!

Create Accountability for Personal and Company Growth

I've had the pleasure to work with many leaders over the years, but Amanda Cunningham is a standout. First, she has the coolest title—I started working with her in 2014 as she took on the role of Continual Improvement Ambassador. During one of our first calls with David, Maria, and Amanda, I knew Amanda was ready to take North Shore to the next level. Her attitude reminded me of the Zig Ziglar quote, "You don't build a business. You build people, and then people build the business." It was very clear that Amanda was ready to own their processes and bring improvements to the team. Her personal sense of accountability is what drove many changes in the coming months, changes that helped North Shore be more effective in empowering their team members through their planning and doing processes.

At the leadership level, they began by increasing their own

accountability to more effective planning and communication. In 2015, they implemented open-book management to better communicate the company financials to the management teams at the various locations. They also ramped up their quarterly planning sessions and the effectiveness of their meetings. "The team really enjoys brainstorming during these meetings," Maria told me. "They're sharing their ideas on opportunities, threats, and Winning Moves. Everybody feels like they are being heard, and we are more focused on solutions." The Start Stop Keep Exercise helped guide their discussions. In fact, it was so successful that they have begun using it during weekly staff meetings and encouraging everybody to discuss their ideas for what they all might start doing, stop doing, or keep doing with their managers. The ideas are put into Rhythm for broader discussion. According to Maria, it has helped bolster collaboration, teamwork, and the idea that everybody is a leader. "As the CEO, I have really benefited from hearing ideas from throughout the organization before we execute any changes."

Measuring priorities and using KPIs—and tracking them weekly—has also helped North Shore promote the right kind of accountability throughout the organization. Amanda said to me recently, "My dad has always told me, 'Asking and getting are two different things.'" That's especially true with performance metrics or KPIs. First, you do have to ask, and a few years ago, North Shore began to do just that. Because profitability driven by the productivity of each therapist was an issue, they established a productivity success metric for each therapist, based on number of visits per week for the type of therapy. "People didn't even know what their productivity expectation was," explained David. "We just weren't managing properly. If you want a performance, growth-oriented culture, people need to know, 'Well, what does the score need to be? And what is the score now?'" This added clarity, along with the hard culture-design work they've been doing for years, has helped increase positivity and proactivity because the transparency is empowering. Two contributors to drama in an organization—and drama can be a culture killer—are subjectivity and lack of candor, which create anxiety because people don't know where they stand.

Just establishing the number helps people focus on what's important, but that's not enough to help them hit the goal. At North Shore, they've taken some big steps to fulfill their promise to clients and employees alike: "Be warmly supported. See change. Blossom!" They are driving the support and collaboration necessary to improve and grow together, and that drives low-drama accountability and empowers their employees to take control of their career. They recognize that's what it takes to make sure the kids are getting the best care possible from engaged, caring therapists.

First, they created what they call a clinical ladder. Therapists can choose to take steps up the ladder toward greater leadership by doing things like writing blog posts, taking on special continuous improvement projects, running a training program for other staff, doing an in-school presentation, and other community relationship–building efforts. Those therapists who say, "I just want to treat kids," don't have to be responsible for activities on the ladder. They can focus solely on meeting their productivity goals, especially now that North Shore has a bigger team, support staff, and management infrastructure to handle other tasks. For therapists who are interested in doing more, though, there are a host of options that help them and the company grow.

The ladder is also a form of support for those therapists who aren't hitting their goals. Each week, the branch managers meet with any therapists who are Red and talk about activities that could improve their productivity, including things on the ladder. They also employ a powerful method that they call "scaling Bright Spots." When they have a therapist who shifts from Red to Green, or who hits Super-Green, they spend time in their weekly meeting to celebrate the success and ask two important questions: What happened in that week that allowed them to be successful? Can we duplicate it going forward? Then, they include what they learn in their discussions with therapists who may be struggling. For those who continue to struggle and aren't particularly interested in some of the ladder activities, they also have the option of moving to a thirty-hour full-time week (rather than forty) or moving to an hourly based pay model.

"We present a lot of options that have proven to help people in the past improve their number or bring it in line with the hours they work, and then let them choose what they want to do. It's just a fact of human nature that if it's something you enjoy doing, you're going to do it more effectively. And the options allow them to say, 'I'm in charge and this is the action I'm going to take.'" When you are supported in your success, accountability doesn't lead to a fear of failure; it leads to feelings of empowerment and engagement.

You can see that same approach in another shift they've made with their meeting rhythms. In 2015, Amanda became laser-focused on determining the best cadence for their annual, quarterly, monthly, and weekly meetings. At first the team was only meeting monthly, and I challenged Amanda to go to the team and propose that they meet weekly. The team hasn't looked back. During this same time, we also created cascade teams in Rhythm so that execution plans would be more visible to the team, and more importantly, more employees could track their related goals and priorities.

Improving your meetings and the desired outcomes should always be a work in progress. Amanda and Maria attended a Rhythm Break-through Conference not long ago and heard a presentation on the power of the Weekly Adjustment Meeting. They realized they needed to make an adjustment of their own. "Just calling it a Weekly Adjustment Meeting was a big win for us," explained David. "It puts you in a different frame of mind. And it also supports our version of the 80/20 rule—spend 80 percent of your time focused on the future and 20 percent on discussing the past." Month by month, I coached Amanda on improving the efficiency and effectiveness of those meetings, so that the team could spend less time talking about the status of a priority and more time discussing the actions they would take to make progress and achieve their growth-oriented goals. To have those productive discussions, all leaders have to status their priorities in Rhythm beforehand, which drives focus and ownership. According to David, the shift has brought more confidence to the team and more leadership-level discussion, and the very nature of the meeting is aligned with their value of focusing on growth and thinking in terms of solutions and results.

The meetings started out as separate for the clinical team and the administrative team, but that has changed, too. Now they meet together so that the changes they consider are aligned with and supportive of the changes happening with other teams, and that has improved communication and collaboration on important growth initiatives, as well as created greater transparency, which helps people feel better about the work.

Recently, one of the therapists went to her branch manager to talk about her progress. Her numbers had been communicated to her each week, and she knew she wasn't hitting the minimum expectation. She took ownership and said, "I know I'm not meeting expectations. Here's what I want to do: I want to switch to an hourly position."

The number of therapists hitting their productivity success levels has increased by almost 30 percent since the first quarter of this year! And staff are increasingly thinking about how to hit the number or how to adjust their situation to align with the level of productivity they're comfortable with. "Our staff is just continuing to exceed expectations," Amanda told me.

10 SIGNS OF A HIGH-PERFORMANCE CULTURE

1. Core values are understood by all and visible in the way people work.
2. Targets and goals are agreed upon as a team in quarterly and annual planning and cascaded to the entire company.
3. Progress and results on priorities and KPIs are transparent and visible at all times.
4. Everyone is clear about what their role is and the results expected of them.
5. Teammates and leaders trust each other to deliver results or ask for help if offtrack.
6. Everyone has the tools and information necessary and feels empowered to create or ask for what is needed.
7. Teams have regular Weekly Adjustment Meetings to review results, work together, and make adjustments.
8. Teammates feel safe and are open to receiving feedback and comfortable sharing it.
9. Cross functional teams share information and work well together.
10. There is an ongoing discussion around personal development and continuous improvement.

Culture by Design Pays Off

"Our topline growth has always continued; we were just becoming less profitable as we were growing," David revealed. "Last year, I wasn't sleeping. But this year, I've been sleeping very well." While revenue growth isn't everything (and David would agree), the leaders at North Shore have been able to use their more than 60 percent topline growth in the past year, produced by their *nine* locations, to develop the resources needed to support greater growth and profitability, all while doing the important culture design work that will continue to support employee happiness.

"Our culture is about service—to our clients and to our employees," David told me. "If they're not happy or they're negative, we have work to do. The most important thing is recognizing the need to actually develop and maintain the culture." And clearly the hard work is paying off. Amanda has said that despite the changes and the challenges of growth, she feels that the culture is the best it's ever been in her seven years with the company. "Allowing people to get into the Green and working with them and strategizing with them on how to get them into the Green if they're not, how to keep them in the Green if they are, it just makes an incredible difference. We've gotten to a point where we have a really positive, supportive culture, where everyone just wants to help each other and the company grow."

It took time for North Shore's leadership and therapists to bring about the culture shift they needed—in fact, it's still happening today. David, Deborah, Maria, and others understand now that a focus on culture is a constant thing, that you should work on it through your Think and Plan Rhythms, that it should be a part of your strategy, and that you should use your processes and systems to bring it to life. The moment you become complacent is the moment it starts to slide in the wrong direction. But with continuous effort to build clarity, transparency, and drama-free accountability, you will maintain an environment that engages and motivates employees, dramatically improves your execution, and helps you continue to grow.

Today, the company is a different place, and the success is obvious. Since 2006, the company has tripled its locations, expanded into other states, incorporated new services, added continuing education for professionals, and more. The end of their tagline is "Blossom!" and that is exactly what they have done.

Big Ideas

→   It isn't easy to sustain a culture in which employee happiness and a drive for growth are given equal importance. Culture is a mix of people and process, and as both of those things change, the culture can evolve in ways that you don't plan or want. You need to design processes and establish systems that put your core values, your purpose, and your desired outcomes into practice weekly, even daily. If you can do that, you will build accountability, engagement, and ownership.

→   A common cause of culture problems is a disconnect or communication gap between the leaders' vision and expectations and those of everybody else. If you haven't communicated those—if you haven't defined your purpose, vision, values, and long-term goals—you aren't sharing the elements for the culture you want. You also need processes and systems that help you bring them to life.

→   Regardless of your values, transparency and alignment can be a crucial part of any good culture building, especially as you grow into a more complex organization.

→   Creating priorities helps a team execute strategic plans to proactively sustain your culture. If your culture needs your attention (and it almost always does), make your focus known and put a stake in the ground. Stay committed. During your planning, make sure the priorities you establish are aligned to support improving elements of your culture. If you don't have priorities for culture, then how will your employees stay focused or know that it is important?

→   Empower your team members through your planning and doing processes. Promote healthy, honest, low-drama conversations about where you are as an individual, a team, and a company—and where you need to be. Two contributors to drama in an organization—and drama can be a culture killer—are subjectivity and lack of candor, which create anxiety because people don't know where they stand.

→ Improving your meetings and the desired outcomes should always be a work in progress. Improving the efficiency and effectiveness of those meetings so that the team can spend less time talking about the status of a priority and more time discussing the actions needed to make progress and achieve your growth-oriented goals will support a solutions-oriented culture.

For tools and insights to help you support a culture of business growth and employee happiness, go to PredictableResults.com.

CHAPTER 11

THE CEO'S PLAYBOOK FOR SUCCESS

How this CEO broke the cycle of firefighting and built a team to confidently navigate the future

Liz McBride

Randy Carr's path to the CEO chair of World Emblem, today one of the largest providers of apparel decorations in the world, wasn't very different from the path of many CEOs of midmarket companies, who are often first-timers. At 25, he inherited the business from his father, who had founded the company and played a key sales role while at the helm. While he'd grown up around the business, he had only been working in it directly for five years, after he had been plucked from college to help save it in a time of trouble. Randy spent his first decade as CEO just holding the company together, feeling the weight of being the guy responsible for 50 jobs and a family legacy he wasn't sure he cared about. Did he really want to pass this pressure and angst on to his kids?

That question, and many others, prompted him to start looking for a path to better growth, revenue, and profit. He needed to ease the pressure and lighten the weight on his shoulders. A self-described extremist, he went out guns blazing. He would ask, "What would Dad do?" and then try to do it better. He toured the competition and bought up the latest technology. He would focus on selling, and then turn around to find that the infrastructure was falling apart. He would drop everything to focus on the infrastructure and then find that sales were slipping. When he was in his office, he focused on handling whatever was in front of him at the moment. "I never had an opportunity to think about passion or core purpose or anything like that," he told me. "Still, I thought I knew what I was doing, that I could do it on my own. Sometimes I was right. More times I was wrong."

Many CEOs of midmarket companies share Randy's experience. They take on the CEO mantle from a family member or after founding a company or being a part of it from the beginning. Some rise to the role after leading a department or division for a few years. One study conducted by PricewaterhouseCooper's Strategy& found that even in large companies, 77 percent of CEOs stepped into the position from within the organization in 2015, which means that most are first-timers.[23] In many cases CEOs like Randy have never been trained for the position and don't know where to spend their time or how to engage their leadership team. But now it's their job and they don't have a boss to offer guidance and feedback. It can be isolating, overwhelming, and a confidence killer. In one report on the experiences of first-time CEOs, one leader said, "When I became the CEO I kept doing the things that got me there. I soon realized that what got me there wasn't going to keep me there. I had a lot of learning to do and I found I was a student without a teacher. That was an awakening."[24]

....

23   Strategy&, "CEO Turnover at Record High Globally, with More Companies Planning for New Chiefs from Outside the Company," April 19, 2016, http://www.strategyand.pwc.com/global/home/press/displays/ceo-success-study-2015.

24   The River Group, *EXCHANGES16: In Conversation with the World's CEOs*, 2016, http://www.trgglobal.com/exchanges.html.

Leaders, especially those who have inherited a business, often lose that loving feeling; they get burned out or uninspired, possibly feel guilty that they're not fulfilling the legacy of their parents or the founders, or feel overwhelmed by the need to meet investors' expectations—or, for CEOs who are founders, feel like they're letting their employees down. Their lack of clarity on how to manage the organization and how to balance their responsibilities often leads to a growth plateau. World Emblem was doing fine, but revenue was stagnating. When leaders are overwhelmed with the fires of day-to-day work and the fear of making a misstep, focus on growth suffers. And so does the leader's confidence.

What most are missing is an operating system that offers a clear definition of the critical role they should play and a path to fulfilling it effectively. If you can relate to even some of this challenge, developing a cadence of thinking, planning, and doing in your leadership approach can make a world of difference by giving you a method to balance working *on* your business with working *in* your business, to engage your leadership team and all your employees, and to establish an inspiring vision and chart a course together. Rhythm is a continuous process that reinforces and builds the critical leadership skills you need—strategic thinking, execution planning, and personal accountability for getting the right work done—to create a company and a team that is ready and excited for what comes next.

At World Emblem, Randy and his team found a path that helped them focus on strategic change rather than the idea of the moment, a drive for steady operational improvements, and a culture of learning, which allowed them to face the brutal facts and then make confident decisions week after week.

Developing a cadence of thinking, planning, and doing in your leadership approach can make a world of difference by giving you a method to balance working on your business with working in your business, to engage your leadership team and all your employees, and to establish an inspiring vision and chart a course together.

You're the CEO, so What's Next?

"I have a Spanish teacher from Cuba," Randy told me. "I asked her, 'How do you live there, with the poverty and the lack of infrastructure and not much freedom?' She said, 'We don't know anything different.'" This was the story Randy told me when I asked him what it was like to lead without a real understanding of what was required of a CEO. He and his team didn't recognize their own dysfunctions, poor communication, or lack of clear plans. "If somebody had come in from the outside who had experienced a very structured organization, they would have said, 'What the hell is going on here?' But if you don't know any better, well . . . Part of growing up in a family business is that you don't know what you don't know."

Randy himself was a victim of "burning-issue syndrome," dropping one thing to jump on the next thing that required his attention. He wasn't sure how to figure out where to focus or what direction to take in his role as CEO. Like many first-time CEOs, he had learned the business from a sales perspective, because that was his father's primary role in the business, so sales probably earned the majority of his attention. Randy's idea of the executive team was anybody who had been with the company for a long time and had influence on the business, which is often the way in midmarket businesses that haven't taken their leadership and management systems to the next level. And despite reading all of Jim Collins's books, he and others on the team struggled to even agree on the difference between vision and mission when they knew they needed one. They kept Googling the terms to try to reach some kind of consensus. (If you're feeling stuck on your core strategy, check out *How Rhythm Helps Companies Go from Good to Great: A Practical Guide for Using Rhythm to Implement Jim Collins's Teachings* at PredictableResults.com.) Most important, they definitely were not making great progress on strategic initiatives, and if they didn't fix that, there wouldn't be a future.

One reason many companies fail is that the founder CEOs or next generation CEOs don't recognize their limitations and their need for guidance. Randy didn't fall into that trap. He knew he and his team needed help, some kind of discipline, and that he needed a system for leading the entire team to the right results.

World Emblem needed an answer to the question, "What's next?" and Randy needed to lead them in finding it by focusing on strategic change rather than chasing one idea or another. They needed a robust core strategy that would help them set a long-range direction, decide where to invest, identify the right market segments, and focus their energy and resources to achieve a set of three-to-five-year goals. But they also needed a system or method for answering the "what's next" question over and over again, week by week, quarter by quarter. Randy felt there were two parts to this question: financial, for which he turned to his profit and loss statement, and operational, for which he turned to the Rhythm playbook.

In late 2011, Randy called us and set the date for his first planning session with a Rhythm consultant. In that planning session, he and his team learned about the annual and quarterly planning rhythms to drive execution of initiatives. Finally, they could start to see a path for setting direction.

At first, though, the World Emblem team definitely faced their share of hurdles—just like many of the executive teams I've worked with before they develop the necessary skills and cadence. "Every ten minutes, one of us was running out of the room. We were fighting about all of the day-to-day problems in the business. Jamie [Randy's brother] and I were arguing about one customer's order. When we started working on a list of priorities, we said, 'We need to work on this, this, this, this, this, this . . .'" They certainly addressed the "what's next" question in their first quarter of planning—but they came up with too many answers. They set *fifty-four* individual priorities for themselves. Granted, many fell under the operational priorities umbrella—what we call day-job versus strategic priorities—but some that were put in that bucket were actually strategic, such as developing new manufacturing performance standards, creating a new incentive and bonus plan, and decentralizing financial reporting. Their Rhythm consultant tried to pull them back from the ledge, but they were sure they would get it all done. "We can do all of it. We got it," Randy remembers the leaders saying. I find that most leadership teams need a learning quarter to begin shifting their thinking about priorities and planning, and that was certainly true at World Emblem.

Randy and his team were confident in their ability to get a laundry list of major projects completed in just three months. Of course, they didn't. "Sure enough," he told me, "the weekly Rhythm meetings were four hours long, everything was Red, we went into the room fighting. The same old stuff." (Except he didn't say "stuff.") The Rhythm methodology and tools didn't instantaneously solve their bad habits, but they did shine a bright light on them.

At that point, some leadership teams might have said, "This is too hard," tucked their heads back into their shells, and moved on to the next "solution" of the moment. Not Randy. He could see the potential of the approach, he accepted the brutal truth of their dysfunction, and he had faith in the potential of the company. So they planned for another quarter. It was better, with slightly fewer individual priorities and more Green on the dashboard at the end. The next quarter was better, and the next, and the next. Gradually, the strategic priorities became more strategic and less tactical and more tied to the long-term plan and vision. Their planning sessions became tighter and more focused. Their Weekly Adjustment Meetings became shorter and shorter, and their discussions became more solution-oriented, maximizing their return on that valuable leadership time. "It took us two years to really adopt the process and get to a decent strategic plan," Randy told me. "Now, we know we have to pick that one thing (the quarterly theme) and nail it. And when we're in the Yellow, when we miss deadlines, it's because the few things we pick are hard and the deadlines we set are tough."

Their company priorities are now often Green, or even Super-Green, because their quarterly plans consistently pass four tests: their *financial* targets for teams roll up to support the company's revenue goal, they pass the *focus* test by having no more than five company priorities, they have the right level of *energy* devoted to supporting the company's top priority each quarter (which I can see when I look at the team and individual priorities tied to each company priority), and each priority has clear and measurable success criteria, which ensures low-drama *accountability*.

The individual teams go a step farther by creating their own Objective Statements each year to define what they need to do to help the company hit annual targets. These Objective Statements result in discussions and alignment on what products to fast-track and programs to adopt in order to retain and attract both customers and employees. Most important, this has helped the team to stop spending energy on ideas, strategies, or products that had been tested but were just not working.

Annually and quarterly, the World Emblem team is identifying the right strategic change and setting a series of inspiring goals that bring the company closer to their Big Hairy Audacious Goal (BHAG) of becoming a $100 million company that is able to see their brands everywhere.

USING AN OBJECTIVE STATEMENT TO FOCUS ON STRATEGY

An Objective Statement is a simple tool that provides a framework and guidelines for working together and making decisions. It might be specific to a project, initiative, or a meeting, or it might be bigger in scope. The purpose of creating an Objective Statement is to ensure that everyone is aligned with the purpose and expectations going forward.

Here is the simple framework:

- TO: What is the action? What are you going to do? Start with a verb.
- IN A WAY THAT: How will you go about doing it? List criteria, scope, involvement, success measures, specific tactics, side benefits, or any other relevant information, but keep it clear and focused.
- SO THAT: Why are you doing this? Why is it important? What is the one main benefit?

As an example, this is what the Objective Statement might look like for World Emblem's executive team:

- TO: Lead World Emblem's teams and individuals.
- IN A WAY THAT: Is aligned around three to five annual initiatives, builds relationships with our core customers, diversifies our product offerings, and attracts and retains A players.
- SO THAT: We hit our annual targets.

Drive Operational Improvements with the Right Team and the Right Rhythms

Speed, quality, service. For any of us, in our work or professional lives, these are the fundamentals of our impression of a company (although mentally, we might occasionally replace speed with something else, like ease of use). At World Emblem, these three factors, plus the likelihood of recommending the company, became the foundation for how they judge their progress on serving customers.

Late in 2013, the team rolled out the new customer satisfaction index (CSI), based on customer ratings of four different factors. In the last three-plus years, their push for excellence on this key performance indicator (KPI) has never flagged. If their overall number from all customers surveyed is 90 or less, that's Red. To hit Green, they have to achieve an overall number of 96—an ambitious goal, especially in manufacturing, where it can be difficult to predict machinery downtime or breakdowns that create a lesser quality product. World Emblem's CSI is not often in SuperGreen, or even Green, but it's not often Red, either. And all of their Yellow weeks prompt them to take action and follow-up with customers who only gave them a seven or eight, when many companies would be happy with that score. "The whole company cares about that number," said Randy, "because we are very vocal about it."

Their customer service team is particularly concerned with their contribution because they receive bonuses based on it. It's about much more than the money, though. At our last planning session, the client services team was one of the Bright Spots the leaders discussed. The team has become even more focused and more responsive to customers over the past year, and has a collective great attitude, remaining true to the number one value of "Stay positive." It is now well known that "You're not going to make it on this team if you're not nice." The best part is it's the team that dictates and enforces this standard. The CSI—reviewed weekly, discussed quarterly, and communicated transparently—has helped create the improvement framework for and the focus necessary to build this culture of positivity.

"Everything we measure and monitor gets attention and that drives incremental change. Things throughout the business have just gotten progressively better." The combined focus on the right key performance indicatos (KPIs) and the right annual and quarterly priorities is driving operational improvements that bring them closer to their BHAG. Over the past two years, for instance, they've been steadily developing and implementing a new enterprise resource planning (ERP) system to integrate systems throughout the company. They are making this investment with their core strategy as their road map, which is crucial because, like all leadership teams, they don't know exactly what World Emblem will look like ten years from now—exactly how big they will be, what lines of business they will have developed, how the needs of their customers may have changed. They return to their core strategy, BHAG, and their notes from their quarterly and annual strategy discussions and use them as a guide. The project highlights Randy's new perspective on confidently leading for the future: "Slow down, plan more, and plan way ahead."

One of the biggest confidence killers for leaders, and most team members, is feeling like you're working hard for little or no progress. A steady flow of success and well-managed change flips that equation and feeds regular boosts of confidence into our daily and weekly work. Recently, Randy said to me, "It's clunky, like ballroom dancing, the first time you try these methods. But you do it over and over and then you look like a professional dancer." The Rhythm approach has given Randy, and others on his team, an essential leadership attribute—confidence that they're focused on the right change at the right time.

With Rhythm, Randy can also feel confident that everybody else knows what's important, what the company is working on, and how they are contributing. Even people who may not have direct access to the Rhythm software are kept firmly in the loop. Randy sends a newsletter out every two or three weeks that includes the top four company priorities for the quarter and their status and company financials. (He ends each letter with a "What I'm Reading" section, where he describes a book and what he's learning from it, which highlights their core value of keeping smart.) Everybody knows what improvements are important to the business.

"I think the trick to business is to be consistently, consistently consistent," said Randy. "No wild swings. The real story of success for the majority of companies doesn't come from chasing the $1.4 billion lottery. It's all about creating a plan, working the plan, and growing at a manageable pace. You unclog one logjam, that reveals another, and then you have to unclog that one. You grow, you set a new plan, and you execute really well quarter after quarter. It gives me confidence to know that we have a game plan that drives this level of focus."

Face the Brutal Facts, Learn From Them, and Take Action

A few years ago, Randy had hired a new, talented IT manager at a time when they needed to revamp their IT infrastructure. In the first quarter, the manager statused Green on all his priorities in Rhythm week after week after week—until the end of the quarter, when he statused every one of them Red. The guy was new and Randy knew the project challenges he was facing. When the new manager explained that this or that had happened to keep him from hitting Green, Randy accepted his explanation. The next quarter, things started off great— one Green week after another. At the end of the quarter, everything was Red or Yellow. And again, Randy gave him the benefit of the doubt. When the same pattern showed up in the third quarter, Randy no longer accepted this performance, faced the brutal fact that the manager wasn't the right fit, and replaced him.

Randy will tell you that it was a learning moment; he felt he should have seen the problem much sooner. He recognizes his own complicity in losing valuable time on key projects: "At the end of the quarter he would be Red and there would be no repercussions. I could be a little too understanding. And I wasn't as clear about the need to use Rhythm. Now when I hire people, I say, 'This is part of the way we run this company. If you want to work here, this is something you have to do. It's not negotiable.'"

One of the greatest confidence builders is the predictability that comes from visibility and transparency. Randy was talking with a salesperson not long ago and the salesperson told him, "I'm here on my goal, and I need to be here." No hemming or hawing or trying to avoid the brutal facts. And Randy was able to respond with constructive questions: "You have eight weeks to close the gap. What's your plan? What are your action items each week?" Five years ago— when those types of specific, accountability-driving questions weren't a part of the company lexicon—who knows how Randy would have responded. Who knows if that conversation would have happened before the end of the quarter, when the salesperson missed his target and it was too late to learn and take action.

Creating a winning company requires working through the Think, Plan, Do Rhythms as a team to test ideas and Winning Moves so you can better predict how successful they will be, speeding up and improving your decision-making, and developing stronger plans for execution to complete agreed-upon priorities and make weekly progress as a company. You can't do this successfully if you don't embrace transparency and honest conversations about the brutal facts in front of you. When you are open to those brutal facts, though, incredible learning opportunities reveal themselves.

This same approach to growth in how the company functions is clear in how Randy approaches his own growth as a leader. "I've been bringing in some new leaders recently," Randy told me during a coaching call not long ago. "The thing I keep telling them is, 'Your job is to replace me, to make sure that if I leave for six months, the company is better off when I get back than it was when I was in the building.' Ten years ago, I wouldn't have said that. I was too consumed with my whole ego." Around the time we began working together, Randy had discovered he needed a team that would challenge him, in a way those who had worked under his father might not have. He needed help maintaining the discipline he knew the company needed. And he needed to be a leader who was open to being challenged and open to change.

When you are a growing company, the most constant thing is change. You have to reevaluate the way you do things and your assumptions. You have to work to improve your leadership capacity and management approach over time. To make the best improvements, you have to face brutal facts that are revealed through transparent sharing of information and feedback.

Before our last annual planning session, Randy and I discussed the plan for the meeting. Randy said, "Dude, I already know what the 2017 plan is. I know what we have to do."

"I know you do, Randy," I responded. "But I need you to sit back and let your team have a chance to create the plan. Your team won't own it unless they were part of creating it."

"Okay," he said, without hesitation. "Help me do that. Tell me when to shut up."

I showed up to the meeting with therapy putty for Randy and his team (mostly Randy), to hold their attention while others were sharing. Randy consciously and patiently waited for his team to formulate opinions and thoughts. He challenged them by asking for creative ways to get things done. And he was the final voice in cementing priorities. What a stark difference to the younger Randy, who would have come in, dictated the plan, and then argued about it. At the end of the session, Randy asked, in front of the team, how they could improve the next planning session for the upcoming quarter. I told him getting people back and focused after breaks was an issue, and he turned to the team and said, "Next time, we're back in here on time, ready to go, with our phones off." In addition to therapy putty, I'll bring a bullhorn.

Randy wants to learn and grow, and takes his team along with him on this journey. He can stand firmly on his foundation and lead with more confidence with each floor they build.

From Chaos to Confidence

For Randy, the Think, Plan, Do approach has taken away much of the chaos and complexity of running a large company. It has helped clarify his role and the company's future. And it has helped him find joy in his work.

Before our last annual planning session, I recommended we spend time in the coming year validating their core values and helping bring them to life with real examples of real people in the company. When I sent out the prep work, I asked Randy and his team to think of someone who resembles the best World Emblem has to offer and share a specific story that highlights why. One of the entries that came back was about Randy: "Randy is always making jokes and laughing, but he gets the job done and has a love for this company that no one else can match." I'm not sure that would have been the feedback six or seven years ago.

In the past five years, World Emblem's revenue has grown 40 percent, while they've doubled their headcount with 700 strong today and heavily invested in infrastructure and operational efficiencies. Randy will tell you that he's still frustrated, that he's always frustrated, but it's a very different type of frustration. Now, he feels passionate about the work and what they've achieved because he understands the work that needs to be done and how it drives the results. His frustrations are mostly related to how to keep doing it better. When I asked him what he wanted to improve, he said, "Every year it's something different, right?"

Like a lot of young leaders, it took Randy some time to recognize that the success of a company is not driven by the CEO, although the

CEO sets the standard. The real driver of the success of a business is talented people making steady progress on individual strategic priorities. Steady progress requires the right team members, the right rhythms to create focus and alignment, and the right discipline to grow personal and team accountability. Recently, Randy said to me, "None of this works if my team doesn't work it."

Since beginning down the Rhythm path, World Emblem has increased their manufacturing footprint by a magnitude of six. They've launched three new noncore brands. And they have become very clear about what they need to do strategically to achieve their BHAG. "The most clear thing I can point to that's different in the company, beyond the products or the plants," Randy said, "is the way it's maturing. Having a solid strategic and planning foundation and taking the time to review quarterly is maturing the team and the organization."

Using Rhythm, World Emblem now has great discipline and a well-defined business execution system, and the company is competing faster, better, and cheaper. The leaders and teams are growing market share and revenue quarter by quarter while setting the company up for a long, profitable future. Randy's wisdom on making it all happen? "You don't need to do these things, to have these rhythms or systems, to run a business. But you do need them to run a business well."

The Big Ideas

→ Leading a company to grow is an incredibly difficult job, and few CEOs are given the tools and training they need to do it well from the start. What most need is a management operating system that creates the focus, alignment, and accountability they know they need but can't seem to build or maintain.

→ Rhythm reinforces the critical skills—strategic thinking, execution planning, and personal accountability for getting the right work done—that leaders need to create a company and a team that is ready for growth.

→ Steady, consistent improvement is the best path to long-term, sustainable growth. When a CEO can build this into the management approach throughout the company, it takes the pressure off every leader to react to the next new idea. Instead, teams become proactive.

→ Being fearless about facing the brutal facts and being open to making necessary, important adjustments is an absolute requirement in leadership today. Having a system that helps reduce fear in the executive team by building transparency, alignment, and low-drama accountability can make all the difference.

→ Leadership confidence comes from clarity on strategy, transparency of results, open conversations about what can be learned from the brutal facts, and clear responsibilities and accountability.

For tools and insights to help you build confidence in your team and your leadership, go to PredictableResults.com.

RESOURCES

To download the tools used by the companies in the book, visit **PredictableResults.com** and use the access code R123PR.

Tools by Chapter

→ Chapter 2: Brand Promise Tool

→ Chapter 3: Opportunities & Threats Tool, Winning Moves Tool, Winning Moves Planner Tool

→ Chapter 4: Breakthrough to Green Tool

→ Chapter 5: *5 Steps to Creating a Winning Annual Plan* Guide, Destination Postcard Exercise

→ Chapter 6: 13-Week Dashboard Tool

→ Chapter 7: Job Scorecard Tool

→ Chapter 8: KPI Creator Tool, Leading Indicator Creator Tool, *KPIs to Drive Your Business* Guide

→ Chapter 9: 13-Week Dashboard Tool, "How to Get Your Team to Execute Faster than the Competition" Webinar

→ Chapter 10: Core Values Discovery Tool

→ Chapter 11: *How Rhythm Helps Companies Go from Good to Great: A Practical Guide for Using Rhythm to Implement Jim Collins's Teachings*

ABOUT RHYTHM SYSTEMS

In 2006, two successful serial entrepreneurs, Patrick Thean and Cindy Praeger, launched Rhythm Systems to help growing companies achieve their dreams and goals.

Today, Rhythm Systems has helped companies across all industries improve team execution, accelerate growth, and achieve predictable results with a lot less drama and chaos. We do this with a simple system that helps companies get more initiatives done successfully.

The Rhythm System provides companies with cloud-based business execution software along with expert consultants to help teams establish the right habits to build accountability with less stress. The result? Business initiatives and long-term success are achieved—every year and every quarter.

What Makes Rhythm Unique?

→ **Our Easy-to-Use Software.** It's not a new process. Input the same information you currently put into your clunky spreadsheets. Rhythm software will create beautiful dashboards for your executive team and departments to organize information and create a collaboration space so your team will stay on track every year, every quarter, every week, and every day.

→ **Our Expert Consultants.** Our Rhythm consultants make the Rhythm System work for you quickly. Rhythm experts have run midmarket companies or have executive experience, so they are quick to understand your needs and bring immediate high value to your organization. Think of it as white-glove service.

→ **Our Fast-Track Implementation.** Most implementations are a nightmare. Not the Rhythm System. With the help of your Rhythm Consultant, your team will be up and running at your next weekly meeting.

→ **Our 100 Percent Focus on the Midmarket.** This is our specialty. We understand the unique challenges of midmarket companies, and our team has a robust set of relevant patterns and experience to help you make better business decisions.

→ **Our Core Values.** We consider our clients a part of our Rhythm family, and our core values are one of the top reasons clients enjoy working with us. We work with them through their challenges and celebrate with them in their success.

- Go the Second Mile
- Keep Smart
- Family Is a Blessing
- Be Appreciative
- No Thinly Disguised Contempt

Questions about the book or the tools?

We'd be delighted to hear from you. Contact us at (704) 209-7290 or PRBook@rhythmsystems.com.

Looking for more?

If you loved *Predictable Results*, you'll love our first book, *Rhythm: How to Achieve Breakthrough Execution and Accelerate Growth*, available on Amazon. For bulk orders, visit RhythmSystems.com.

To book one of the authors for a speaking engagement, contact us at speaking@rhythmsystems.com.

ABOUT THE AUTHORS

Patrick Thean is a successful serial entrepreneur. He grew Metasys, Inc. to number 151 on the Inc. 500 and received the Ernst & Young Entrepreneur of the Year Award for North Carolina. Today he is the CEO of Rhythm Systems and the architect behind Rhythm software. Patrick received his Master of Engineering degree from Cornell University. He speaks to thousands of business people globally every year to help them achieve breakthroughs in their strategies, execution, and team performance.

Chris Cosper is an expert in creative problem-solving with a passion for helping others bring their visions to life, whether working with business leaders or serving on nonprofit boards. After eight years as a leader and CEO of a children's apparel manufacturer, she joined a consultancy focused on developing corporate culture as a driver for success. As head of consulting at Rhythm Systems, she oversees the work the team does daily to help clients achieve their goals and dreams.

Alan Gehringer's passion for helping companies succeed is rooted in his experience growing up in a family manufacturing business. After returning and reengineering the business model to improve sales and profitability, he then ran the business successfully for years. Leveraging his engineering degrees and MBA, he has helped start up and reengineer other midsize businesses, and he became the CEO of a public-private partnership that helped companies develop innovative strategies for profitable growth. Today, he works to help companies of all kinds realize their full potential.

Tiffany Chepul is an expert at simplifying complex concepts. Her consulting firm, Toolshed Partners, helped public relations companies evaluate products and vendors to provide maximum efficiency at the lowest cost. As a sales leader at PR Newswire, she gained insight into marketing and customer relationship management. And as a partner at her family's CPA firm, she provides input on strategic planning and operations. She loves diagnosing issues and motivating teams to action. Her entrepreneurial spirit has helped her launch the Rhythm Certification Program and grow the community of certified members.

Barry Pruitt has an oversized passion for great people and great leadership. Barry started his first business at age 8, and first sold a business at age 18. Since then, his almost three decades as a leadership development expert, working with organizations such as FedEx, Ford Motor Company, NASA, and Walt Disney Imagineering, have helped him build deep insight into best practices across industries and around the world, which he uses to help companies and leaders grow.

Cathy McCullough's passion is working with leaders of organizations of all sizes and sectors to transform their companies. As an organizational culture expert, she works with leaders to identify their strategic intent, build higher performance cultures, and increase their leadership effectiveness. She is a seasoned speaker, having presented at national and international conferences. She has published or been featured in numerous news publications, graduate textbooks, *TD* magazine (a publication of the Association for Talent Development), and *Forbes*.

Liz McBride is a change thought leader, working with leaders to help prepare and shape their teams to optimize growth. She brings an energetic, fun-loving spirit to her work with clients and has an innate ability to read the room. With Silicon Valley chops as a Google Deployment Specialist and Salesforce Administrator, Liz led a change practice to develop tools and move global organizations to the cloud. A dynamic speaker for both leadership and autism inclusion, Liz ignites her passion to find creative ways to tap into everyone's inherent gifts to maximize growth potential.

Ted Skinner is passionate about disrupting the status quo and is fascinated by the rapid pace of technological change and innovation. Balancing his technical aptitude with his drive for team growth, he helps leaders develop revenue growth strategies. During his fourteen years as a software executive with PR Newswire, he won the prestigious John Petrillo Award for the employee most dedicated to customer service. Ted loves helping his clients achieve their business goals with breakthrough execution.

Melissa Enriquez's education as an engineer and her fascination with human interaction combine to give her unique insights into execution excellence. As an executive for an Inc. 5000 tech-services company, she managed strategic planning and execution efforts designed to connect with customers' needs and employees' motivations. Her persistent, methodical approach has helped many leaders tackle the challenges of growth.